SOLD

By

Billy Williams

SOLD
A LIFE STORY

ISBN: 978-0-578-37375-1

FIRST EDITION PAPERBACK

First Printing 2021

Printed in the United States of America
Library of Congress Cataloging in Publication Data on file.

Published by
Circle Square Services
Corona, California
circlesquareservices.com

For Momma Carrie
...love is patient...
&
Daddy Bill
...love is kind...

Foreword

Truth comes when you least expect it. For me, it came with a phone call to a woman named Shelbi Walker. I had been referred to her from a dear friend who had used her services in the past. I, as you will soon learn in detail, was in search of my biological roots. My friend, who was adopted, hired Shelbi and her organization, GRAITH Foundation, to assist in locating her biological family. My friend told me that if anyone could help me solve my family mystery, Shelbi could, and she did. I acknowledge Shelbi and the GRAITH Foundation here, first, because without her, my story would still be untold, and this book would not be in your hands. Ten-thousand thank yous to every member and worker on her team, for taking your precious time to find the pieces of my life that have allowed me to complete my story. Shelbi, your Foundation provides a much-needed service in our world today.

I would also like to thank you, the reader. You are embarking on a journey through my life that has had unexpected twists and turns. My life story is filled with tragedy and triumph. I tell it to you so that you will hopefully be able to see yourself through the lens of my life and how everything that you go through is meant for your good. I know you've heard that before, but the truth is, God has a bigger plan for your life than you can even imagine, and everything you go through -- the good and the bad -- is meant to draw you closer to Him and fulfill your greater purpose for His kingdom. Your story matters, and my desire is that you will find a space and place to begin to speak and write and share your truth.

I wrote this book with that in mind, in fact. I wanted to speak and write and share my truth with the world. My reasons were selfish, at first. I wanted to get things off of my chest and "wipe the slate clean." After the first paragraph, however, I realized that my words weren't just for me, they were for you. The fact of the matter is that I wanted to make sure that every person who is drawn to this book and brave enough to open its pages, did so for a reason. Perhaps you have felt alone, rejected, abandoned, or unloved like I did for so many years. Maybe you are in search of your identity. Or could it be that you feel like you've been lied to, and you don't know the truth about your life. I wrote this book for you. You are in a safe space between these pages, and I am encouraging you to read to the end, this story and your own life story. Don't skip ahead or drop the book in the middle. It gets better, I promise. Just stay the course and keep going. It may seem tough, unbearable even, it may seem hard or completely impossible, but the truth is, the situation you are in can work out for the good! I am a living witness and example that anyone can make it no matter their circumstances.   Through this reading, I pray to provide answers and solutions that will assist anyone in handling the gut punches life has to offer. We don't have to be stuck feeling hopeless with no way out.

What you are about to read is based on real

events that happened to me. Everything is true as I remember, and I have recounted each story to ensure that the privacy of my family and friends is respected. My intention is to share **MY** story, not to harm anyone else.

My prayer is that you will be filled with joy, living in your purpose with the peace of God in your heart. You must find your inner strength and come to a true understanding that your life matters. For those of you that don't believe in God, that's OK, this book is still for you. Don't let that be the reason that you don't keep reading. If you're mad at God, keep reading anyway! Look beyond our God differences and share in my story, as an average, plain, human being. Hear me out, and after, you can still feel however you want about God. I couldn't tell my story without Him, and I can't truly live my life without Him. I will offer this, however, if you are looking for answers and you see no way out of your situation, God is a great place to start. Begin with prayer and then, take a hard, honest look at yourself. My hope is that what you see is what God sees in you as His beloved child. If He brought you to it, He will bring you through it. Be willing and open to receive Him and watch your world expand.

5

Introduction

The fact that you are reading this right now, means we did it! You can't imagine how long it took me to get started writing my memoir, and to muster up the courage to share my story. I had a continual tape that played in my head telling me to keep my story to myself. It discouraged me and caused me to become easily distracted when I was determined to write. It showed up as a shiny object in the corner or a overly, heavy schedule. It was cunning and calculated. It convinced me that no one wanted or needed to hear my life story. I'm not a celebrity or anyone of note. I'm just a regular guy with an extraordinary life. On my worst days, I succumbed to the crafty ways it spoke to me. Other days, I would be left alone because I was too embarrassed or distraught to write. That's one thing I have learned about the enemy -- he only bothers you when you are walking and doing what the Lord has commanded you to do. He does not care about you when you are lazy or distracted. Have you had your spirit stirred up, and the moment you begin walking in the gifting that God has given you, it seems like all hell breaks loose? This breaking is exactly that; it is a trick of the enemy to keep you from doing what you've been called to do. Don't fall for it!

For 3 years, I was tripped up by the sly nature of the enemy. When I finally got serious and courageous enough to pen these words, he threw everything at me -- work, opposition, a lack of time, and then, in March 2020, a global pandemic. But as always, what the enemy means for bad, God will turn it around for my good. Sitting in quarantine for months allowed me time to reflect on my life and, more than anything, it gave me the time and confidence to begin writing. By that time, I was immune to the constant barrage of, "Don't write this book." "You're a nobody." "Who will listen to you?" And my personal favorite, "Who cares about you?

You're not a celebrity with millions!" I wasn't exempt from those ideas popping into my head, but I knew that my story had to be told, and if I didn't tell it, lives couldn't and wouldn't be changed. Those that are silent would never be heard, and those that were hiding would never be seen. I was obligated to counter that voice and meet it head on, with another one, that I recited daily, "You are strong. You are mighty. Your story matters." I repeated that time and time again until it was to only thing I could hear or see. I then put pen to paper and started writing.

That, I suppose is the first lesson of this book; Listen. Listening to that influence that encourages you and motivates you to do right, to be strong, and to persevere is the beginning of your whole life transformation. In the psycho-social world, they call it "self-talk." What you say to yourself, about yourself, will manifest. The Bible says that there is, "power of life and death in the tongue," and that "as a man thinketh, so he is." No truer words have ever been spoken. Getting out of my own head and attuning my ear to God's commands has allowed me to not only write, but live an abundant, wonderfully complex life.

Throughout this book, I will be offering you nuggets of wisdom based on what God gave me through a particular situation. Underline these little things that I'll be sharing. They are the secrets to living a fulfilled, peaceful life. I am rich, not in money, but in true peace and inner joy. When you have a reason to live and enjoy life, this is the formula that defeats the evil that tells you to give up and convinces you that you, nor your story, matters.

I know of what I speak. The idea of listening to God worked for me and helped bring me out of my funk and depression at very critical times in my life. In the recent past, I have learned that the more I shine my own light, the more I am able to see the light in others. Every person has had some sort of adversity to overcome and because of it, their light has been dimmed or extinguished. Sadly, many don't make it through. So many people are turning to drugs, excessive alcohol consumption, crime, and suicide to cope with unaddressed trauma and pain. The rates are alarming for the young and the old and are ever-increasing. People are suffering in silence because they don't think that their issue had been experienced by anyone else. Not so. We are all suffering and it's time to tell the truth so that we can be free.

You must understand, it took me a long time to get to this point, to this realization of mattering. It was hard, it was difficult, and I didn't always listen to that voice that guides and directs me closer to God. When we empower the enemy, and begin ignoring the sweet, still, voice of God, we multiply and magnify the problems that we have, instead of celebrating the grace of God in and through lives. Today, hear me and hear me well, YOU ARE SOMEBODY SPECIAL! YOU HAVE BEEN CREATED IN THE VERY IMAGE OF GOD. YOU, DEAR READER, MATTER. AND YOUR STORY MATTERS TOO! So, despite my hard head and slow thinking process and your resistance to crack open this book, we are here, and we did it! Hallelujah. Enjoy.

CHAPTER ONE

White

My name is Billy Williams. Well, this is who I thought I was. My life, as I knew it, began the son of two loving parents, Daddy Bill and Momma Carrie. They were a well-to-do, childless Black couple, living in Los Angeles. My Father, Daddy Bill, was a heavy, powerful specimen of a man. He was a hulking figure. When he entered a room, everyone would sit up a bit straighter and take notice. His stature was intimidating, but under it all, he was, in my eyes, a sweet, open, loving man. I didn't know a lot about his upbringing, but as an adult, I have been able to research his family. It is a great gift to give yourself to learn about your history. The ancestors have so much to say, and I have found that exploring their lives can unlock mysteries in our own.

William "Bill" Williams was born on December 25, 1910, in Texas. His Mother, Beulah Roberson, was a mysterious figure. Little is known about her or her family. Even less is know about my grandfather. I don't even know his name. Truthfully, I don't know the answers to a lot of questions related to my life or family. These questions don't enter the mind of a person surrounded by a family who looks like them, having the same facial features or mannerisms. I didn't have a family heritage with stories passed down, nor land and wealth inherited. I don't have any of that. My life, as I knew it, was lived in the shadow of truth and I was merely a mirror of what was around me, rather than a truth that lived in me.

In my story, you will see that truth is relative. My truth could've caused me to become bitter and angry about being lied to or excluded from what is rightfully mine, but instead, this book is a celebration of the sovereignty of God and the fact all things happen at His Divine time. That is the point of this book. Understanding and surrendering to God's timing. My life is wonderful, not because I'm rich with mansions and Bugattis, but because I'm free. My truth has set me free, and my prayer is that you too will find the freedom that you seek. Not knowing the answer to life's questions can affect a person's entire existence and challenge their ability to find a place in the world.

I believe there is a difference between a person blessed to be raised with their biological family and others searching for answers. I had a wonderful childhood, however, that doesn't change the fact that I always knew that I didn't fit. Biological children, raised by their parents have the benefit of knowing where their eyes come from or why they walk the way they do. People like me wonder. I always felt like a square peg in a round hole. I didn't know why; I just knew that it didn't fit. Children raised by their biological parents know who they come from, good or bad. Sharing life with your birth family doesn't exempt you from pain or betrayal. It gives you a sense of knowing. I was told by many people that they have been hurt by their own blood family more than people outside their bloodline. This trips me out. You would think your blood family would do everything in their power not to hurt you, not to take advantage of you. With your biological family, there is no mystery with your blood family, nothing to wonder, you kinda know what to expect. I call it the Benefit of Biology. Whether your family is good or bad, at least you KNOW that they are your family. The benefits can be knowing that there is a tribe to call your own, having well-established family traditions or stories, having heirship, and just the benefit of having a history. The benefits can also be unsavory like a history of drug or alcohol abuse, mental health issues, or physical health issues. Though it seems daunting, knowing your roots, even the bad stuff, is healing. But what if you don't know? Then what?

Every time I go to the doctor, the prescreen nurse asks me, "Do you have any family history of _______________?" Put any condition in the blank. My answer, each and every time, was the same. *"I don't know."* Every. Single. Time. The simplest of things that every human being should know, I didn't. My stomach would drop. I was constantly reminded that I didn't have a root. I was untethered, flailing like a wayward flag. My mind would start to compute to find answers, and I always hit a wall in the thinking process. *"I don't know."* It was a horrible feeling. For this reason alone, I believe that it really helps knowing where you come from, I'm sure of it. Although this is true, it doesn't mean you can't make it in life without knowing your biological family, but there are questions to which you will never have answers unless you venture down the path toward knowing.

These types of questions about my roots hit me at an early age. Many people say they can remember their childhood way back to their threes or fours. I can't. I can, however, remember short bits and pieces of actual events I know occurred, because certain parts of my memory have stored them like a bank vault.

When I was four, I got a puppy, a beautiful White toy poodle. I loved this dog. He was so loving and joyful, but, where she came from, I can't answer that, and I can't tell you what day I got her. However, I knew she was real because I remember her peeing everywhere and Momma got mad at me like it was my fault. This puppy was so excited to see me, and everybody else, she would wag her tail at 1000 miles per hour, and just pee everywhere. I remember because I was the one that had to clean it up. Momma made me get a bucket, soap, and a rag. I would scrub with my little hands until the carpet was foaming White, then yellow. I remember the smell and the satisfaction I felt when the stain was gone.

I remember, soon after I got that puppy, Momma got me a chicken, which is funny, because we lived in the city. I remember this chicken because it had to have a red light in its cage. I thought the red light was cool. I would just stare at it at times. I learned later that the red light was heated to keep the little chickee from freezing at night. I still don't know what Momma was thinking, because chickens are very messy. There would be seed everywhere and I had to clean it up and change the newspaper all the time. Although Momma was a clean freak, I felt like I was the one cleaning everything.

I think the real reason Momma got me these animals was because she was trying to make me a farmer. She was teaching what she knew. She came from a long line of great farmers from the Midwest. I recall when I was a kid, we would visit my Aunt Gladys and my Uncle Day's house every summer in

Oklahoma. My Aunt told me one time, "I don't want to live in the big city nephew. I am content with my ole' simple country life." My Aunt Gladys was a sweet lady who was also strong-willed. She was soft spoken, but when something needed to be said, she opened her mouth to say it. In those days, adults didn't talk to children often, but during those hot Oklahoma summers, I learned so much about farming from her and her husband. Uncle Day taught me how to sloop hogs, ride horses, and grow vegetables. I had a green thumb when it came to growing collard greens. I guess that's why I love mustard, collards, and turnip greens to this today. All I need is a little cornbread and pot liquor and I am a happy man.

I also learned how to shoot rifles and BB guns. Momma didn't like it and did not allow those things back home in Los Angeles. She said, "Black boys get killed with guns." I remember my Aunt Gladys telling her to let me be a boy and shoot those guns. They went back and forth on that subject for a while. While they bickered, I'd sneak out of the house, line up cans, and have target practice, much to my Mother's dismay. Aunt Gladys didn't understand our different lifestyles. In the Oklahoma, a Black boy could shoot a gun into a country field, and no one batted an eye. Where we lived in Los Angeles, guns weren't used for recreation. People, including the police, would shoot a Black boy to kill. During that time, Momma Carrie had a great point. By the late 1960s, 1970s and 1980s, young Black men were dying at an alarming rate to gun violence. Blacks in L.A. were at war with the cops, White people, Hispanics, and worst of all, Blacks were at war with each other. Black-on-Black crime was huge then, and is still an ongoing issue in our communities. I never understood why. It seems a particular group of people should stick together, not eliminate one another. But if you're taught to hurt your own people, I guess that's what you do.

From my understanding Momma's family was a prominent Black family in Oklahoma, by way of North Carolina. I was often told that my great grandfather was a wonderful preacher/teacher that helped many learn to read and fed families all over North Carolina. The family also had acres and acres of land and grew vegetables and raised cattle, hogs, chickens, and goats. Makes sense about Momma and that chicken, right?

The highlight of my annual summer trips to Oklahoma was spending time with my cousin, Chelle. She looked and acted more like a sister to me. She was the daughter of my Aunt Clara Luper. Author of *"Behold the Walls,"* Aunt Clara was one of the first Black women to run for the United States Senate in Oklahoma, and she was a staunch Civil Rights activist. She and my Mother had grown up together and their friendship remained strong until Momma's death in 2001. Clara even mentioned Momma and I in her book.

When Aunt Clara was running for the U.S. Senate, we helped with her campaign. I gathered signatures and I was a greeter. I would be at the front door smiling and thanking people for coming, then I would tell them to vote for my Aunt Clara. She was very serious when it came to education especially reading. She pushed me to read anything and everything that would increase my knowledge. She taught me that if I could read, I could be free and have no limitations. A person that could read, can learn to do anything. Her words and inspiration caused me to think more seriously about my education. Every year when she saw me, she would ask if I knew what college I was going to attend. From the age of 8, until I graduated from Crenshaw High School she asked. She truly felt knowledge was power. Her activism has been noted all over the world. Aunt Clara was involved in the sit-ins of the 1950s and 1960s. Having her show me the strength and fight a person needs to have to survive in life, was a blessing to me.

Although Aunt Clara was impressive and pushed me toward success, nothing in Oklahoma was more wonderful than Chelle. She was so much fun! She was light-skinned, just like me, and I felt comfortable around her. We were both "light brights." I hated that term. When I alone, and someone called me that, I felt like the odd man out. Black people didn't like me because I was too light and White people didn't like me because I was too Black. When I was with Chelle, I felt normal, accepted, and understood.   The idea of colorism is real and by design. Somewhere, in the basement of history, lies the divide and conquer approach to Blackness. Some European person decided that separating us by skin hue would destroy us from the inside out and the crack of a whip would no longer be needed because we would kill ourselves instead. Chelle and I both looked White, and we both experienced pain and suffering from our own people about the complexions that we could not control. We bonded over our shared sadness and lack of acceptance.

Because my skin is so White, people called me names all my life. Everyone, even my own family, called me names like, light bright damn near White, White boy, milk, sugar, Casper the Friendly Ghost, and *wigger*. I was called poor White trash by Black people. People didn't know what or who I was. I wasn't White enough to be White, nor was I Black enough to be Black. I was a pale skinned, nondescript human being with no sense of identity. The story began with my skin and ended in my soul. Little did I know that those Oklahoma summers would be the catalyst for me to discover my truth.

When I was 5-years old my parents took me to the Bill Pickett Rodeo in Oklahoma. Bill Pickett was a well-known Black cowboy born in Texas. Every year, there would be a big rodeo in Oklahoma to honor him.

The rodeos in Oklahoma were so much fun. The food, the animals, the cowboy hats, and boots. Everyone donned Western wear. I was intrigued by the clowns that stopped the bulls from hurting the bull riders. I even liked barrel races. I loved to see it all. The horses going full speed trying not to knock down the barrels and the bull riders trying to stay on for eight seconds. The rodeo became a summer highlight for me.

There I was, at the rodeo, having a great time. I looked up into the massive crowd, and I didn't see anyone I knew. I was lost and terrified. Everyone looked the same -- they were all Black. There I stood, this little White skinned boy, lost among people that look like my people, but are not. I wept. I remember feeling this sense of abandonment. *They left me. Why did they leave me?* I don't remember too many details, however, I do remember finding the police. I must have gravitated towards them because they were light like me. Whatever the case, they took me to the announcer's booth, and they passed me over to the Black people in the booth. The Black announcer said, "We have this little White boy, and he is lost." My own people called me White. My reaction was quick, "I ain't White!" The announcer was stunned. He apologized for his error saying, "My bad little man. I'm sorry. We cool?" I stared at him long and hard, with my 5 year-old eyes, and said, "Yeah. We cool." There is something about that moment that stuck with me. It was one of my first experiences dealing with the fact that people don't know what race I am. I started to ask myself who am I? Am I Black or am I White? I truly didn't know.

CHAPTER TWO

Bibles, Belts, Secrets, and Lies

At 5, God put a calling on my life. He was preparing me for something. I'm sure of it now, but didn't know then. As a small boy, I would go to convalescent homes to care for elderly people's feet and legs. Momma would make a kit with alcohol, witch hazel, and lotion and then she would drive me to the homes. I washed and moisturized the feet and legs of the patients. I never considered it gross or embarrassing. I enjoyed seeing the faces of the residents who felt some needed relief. My Mother reminded me that I was doing God's work and in doing so, I was mimicking the ways of the Lord. I beamed with pride at the thought that God was pleased with me.

God has always been a part of my life. I'm drawn to that feeling of connection to His Holy Spirit. I have always wanted to continue feeling His joy. Even after making wrong turns and poor choices, I would cry out to the sky asking for that joy to replace the shame and guilt that I felt. Ever since I could remember, bishops and ministers would come to town and stay at our house. I remember their many visits because I had to give up my bed and room to accommodate them. I didn't mind because I got to sleep on the couch or the living room floor and watch TV before falling asleep.

For decades, Momma cooked for the AME church, serving and hosting ministers who would travel to Los Angeles to preach or attend a conference. I had a front row seat to great conversations between all the ministers sitting at my dinner table. My ear was attuned to them speaking, and I hung on every word. Often, I would mimic their tone to sound like a preacher. They were intelligent men who could turn one phrase into an entire sermon. I marveled at the noise and chatter that was in the house during those visits. I never wanted them to leave.

Since I was an only child, I always remember being alone. I was always alone so these encounters were fuel to my empty, starving heart. Truth is, I had to deal with myself. I don't mean in a negative way. I enjoyed being by myself and I often talk to the objects that I was playing with, creating skits and acting them out all by myself. I would be a teacher teaching students. I would be a fireman putting out fires and saving people. I would be a preacher preaching to the congregation. I imagined myself as a football player running for touchdowns. My imagination ran wild. I had a lot of conversations with God, and often, I could hear Him speaking to my spirit. For a long time, I thought that I was crazy because I could actually feel His spirit come over me when I prayed to Him. I have come to realize that it is a pleasure and a delight to feel the presence of God in you. I knew God early in my life and He hasn't stopped speaking to my yet.

I have always had a sense of service to help people or do things for others. Early in my childhood, I protected the kids that were being teased. I stood up for what was right. Despite all that I knew to be right, I ended up not living the life God had called me to live. I chose, on many occasions throughout my life, to follow my own desires instead of God's Will. At one point, I started to tease others before they teased me, or after they started teasing me. I was not the saint I appeared to be. I was a great fence rider. I did terrible things, I hurt people and made awful decisions. I was an angry, violent man. I was a perfect example of being lukewarm. I lived my life with one foot in, and one foot out my Christianity. You know what I mean, Godly in front of those you know, and then act however you please with reckless abandon around people that accept your evil ways. Every time I've been disobedient to God, it has added consequences to my life. I had to learn God is everywhere and we can't hide from Him.

The cool part about my early childhood was that I had everything a child could want. Momma took real good care of me, and my Dad provided everything that we wanted and needed. In a child's eye, it felt like we were ballin'! My life was off the hook. I had bikes with training wheels, TVs, games, basketball courts, kites, remote control cars, and my favorite toy was my Big Wheel. I parked it in front of our house like it was

Cadillac! Not only did I believe that we were millionaires, but Momma also dressed me like we were millionaires. I was always dressed sharp, donning the latest styles and shopping at expensive department stores. I never questioned or asked how we were able to afford such luxury. I simple basked in the abundance.

When I was in kindergarten, my life took a dramatic shift. The comfort of my blissful existence made a turn, and I lost a bit of innocence in one fail swoop. I remember playing in the school yard after a class session. Maybe it was before school started, I'm not sure. I can't remember the conversation between me and my classmates or what we were talking about, but before I knew it, I was confronting a bully that was bothering another child. The bully swiftly turned his attention to me and said, "You ain't Black! You White! Why are you so White?" My little mind stumbled to try to understand why he would think that I was White. The announcer at the rodeo had thought that, now this kid too? I didn't understand why my skin color was always questioned and the subject of ridicule. I knew this kid and we had played together before and everything. I thought we were the same. I was told Black folks come in all shades. I lived in a Black neighborhood, with Black parents, and Black friends, and I went to a Black church. As far as I was concerned, I was Black!

After that encounter on the playground, I started to question my identity. I didn't know what it was to be Black because everyone around me said that I was White. What is a Black life? Was my Blackness defined by the slang terms that rolled off my tongue, or the dip in my walk. I watched Black shows like the *Jeffersons, Good Times, What's Happening, Soul Train,* and my favorite show, *Sanford and Son.* I loved Black music, especially Gospel. Black music was the soundtrack of my life. Momma would play Aretha, Nat King Cole, and all the Motown greats. I dressed like a Black person with a little extra swag that comes naturally. I patterned my look after the people in my family and TV influences. I wanted to wear clothes like people at my church and actors like Billy D. Williams, Sidney Poitier, and sports figures like Muhammad Ali. I was Black. I loved eating collards and cornbread, and experienced life through the lens of my Blackness. I was a Negro child, a little Black boy regardless of my skin color and despite what people thought. I have lived long enough to be called an African, African American, spear chucker, person of color, jigga boo, darky, porch monkey, colored, Negro, Nigger, and nigga.

My life was Black. Everywhere I went there were Black people. My church, my barber, stores, and my family were all Black, but now, that was all being challenged by this little boy. Everything I thought I knew about myself became hazy. I started to question who I was. Why am I so White? I also realized that I had anger issues because of the way I reacted to his comment. I was enraged. I responded to his remark saying, "Why you so ugly?" He replied, "You a honky!" My rage overtook me, and I blacked out. To a Black man, having your race called into question is one of the worst things that can happen in life, even for a 5-year-old. Why? Because our Blackness is our identity. Even with slavery, inequality, and a corrupt justice system geared to keep people of color down, out and locked up in prisons, being Black is a privilege. We are, despite what the world says, proud to be Black and calling us anything else is an insult. Plus, I'd heard this term many times in conversations before at my dining room table and knew it was not a good name to be called. Even on *All In The Family*, Mr. Jefferson called Archie Bunker a honky. It was derogatory. So, without any spinach at all, I commenced to whooping that kid's ass like Popeye would whoop Brutus. I swung and swung until the playground teacher came and pulled me off of him. It was reactionary. Where I grew up, you either survive or die. You learn early that sometimes you gotta run and sometimes you gotta fight. That day, I chose to fight.

Being the dutiful Christian Mother she was, Momma Carrie made it swiftly to school with a Bible in one hand, and a belt in the other. When she arrived, I was in the office with a red face, bloody knuckles, and not a scratch on me from the other kid. She looked into my eyes with disappointment and a healthy dose of her own rage, and then she whooped my butt in front of everybody. She whooped my butt all over the school yard. She didn't care that I had been called a honky or was teased, she only cared that I handled the situation wrong. As she is whooping me all the way home, I got an ear beating and heard sermons, mid-swing. She was saying, "Boy, you can't be this way, you are special. God has a calling on your life." She preached all while beating my butt. In my head, all I cared about was the licks that she was freely giving out. They really didn't hurt, but they were so embarrassing. The kids teased me about it for months. "Your Momma whooped your butt!" was all I heard for years. I laughed about it because, she did.

No matter what my Momma said to me, at that time, I knew I was different. My whole being was in question. First, I noticed that my skin was whiter than everyone in my family, even the light-skinned blacks were darker than me. I knew, instinctively that there was no way in hell I was a product of my caramel complected Mother and mocha complected Father. My Dad was darker than my Momma, and I was White. White. White. Second, and probably most importantly, I was special. God had a plan for me. I knew it in my soul, even at 5-years-old, that I was chosen to do something great. I didn't know what it was going to be, but I knew deep down that it would change the world. Third, I learned very early in my life that my actions had consequences. That day, I learned that I had to act differently than the way I had just behaved because God was watching me. As a teen and as a young adult, I struggled with this truth because I wanted to do what I wanted to do. I believe that those that who are chosen by God to do His work, are always met with a fork in the road. My road was often rough because of the choices I made, but I still believed that my path was already laid out for me -- the good and the bad.

The truth is that fight on the playground was just the beginning of the battles that I had to wage in my youth and throughout my adulthood. My opponent, however, shifted one day from a small child to a grown-up. On one of our trips when I was about 6 or 7, we went to the East Coast. It wasn't Oklahoma. I know that because of all the city lights I saw. I knew we were in a different place because the flight took forever, and I had been to Oklahoma several times and knew that the flights were shorter. Momma said we were going to visit some family. That's all I knew.

On that fateful trip, I was violated by an older man. The details and the identity of the abuser are unimportant. In fact, I only share this story to give you the power to speak your own truth, and to let other victims know that they are not alone. I will not feed the story another morsel of my being by outlining the who's and what's and when's of what happened. Just know that that moment changed my life forever. I was confused. The twisted thing about the sexual abuse of a child is the betrayal that you feel inside. Your mind knows that it is wrong, but your physiological response tricks you into believing that there's something right and pleasurable about the experience. Abusers know this, and they will use the physiological to justify their abuse. I was a child. I felt guilty and had to live with that for decades. My innocent mind had been corrupted and my playful soul died a bit that day. I never saw that man again and I am sure he has violated others before and after me. Tragically, at 6-years-old I have seen and felt the worst of the worst. On the outside, my life was perfect and beautiful, but on the inside, a rage was beginning to form and soon, it would erupt.

I have always liked girls. I remember sitting in the sand with a little girl admiring he smile, her deep brown skin, and her playful laugh. I remember playing jump rope with the girls and could double dutch with the best of them. Just to see the girls jump up and down over that rope was exhilarating. For hours on end, I would play hopscotch and jacks just so that I could be around the girls. After I was violated, I was confused and had no one to turn to for help. I had done these sexual things with a man at 6, and now I must deal with those feelings and wanting that feeling again. I didn't know how to process it all. The constant self-talk that I did centered around the question of whether I should like girls and boys, or just girls, or just boys? These questions loomed in my head for years. Not only was I questioning my parentage, now, because a sick twisted man violated me, I was questioning my sexuality.

I was angry because this lady who was supposed to be my Mother, charged with loving and protecting me, allowed this man to do these horrible things to me. Where was my protection? Up until that incident on the school yard, I never saw a difference in my skin color associated with being Black and now that incident with that man called into question everything I knew about being a man.

The challenges that I had with colorism were ever present and the molestation sat right at the surface of my soul every day. I was able to hide it from those around me and pretend that it hadn't happened. I compartmentalized my trauma to protect my sanity. My skin, however, was out there for all the world to see. Color was defining in my community. Almost everyone around me was darker than I was. My Mother, Father, preachers, the actors I wanted to dress like, the action stars I admired, were all dark in skin tone. I was surrounded by dark-skinned people. I still did not realize that I was different until it was brought to my attention that day on the playground. Before that fight, I believed that I was Black, and therefore I was Black to everyone else too. My beliefs were being questioned and my identity was teetering, ready to crash like a stone off a cliff. Now, as a grown man, I marvel at the power of the mind. It has the capability to avoid, transform, and rewire a particular memory to shape it to fit comfortably in your brain, creating whatever narrative we subscribe to. With your mind, you can do and be whatever you choose. Nobody has control over your mind.

I started to believe that there was something wrong with me. My questions to my Mother were often met with runaround or the occasional response of, "Don't bother me about this" or "I'm your Mother and I feed you, I clothe you, and I provide everything you need, so don't worry about that stuff." I didn't have the vocabulary at the time, but I now know that she was deflecting. Her answers were to dismiss my concerns and reframe the narrative to her care and concern for me, rather than helping me discover my identity. I've always been smart, so I knew that was bull crap. What we need to learn here, and what Mommas all over the world should know — stuff doesn't complete a person. We as children are keenly aware when you we are lying to us or when you are trying to throw us off the scent of truth. I was astute enough to recognize my Mother's hesitance, but my questions persisted even more. She finally got to the point where she gave in to my questions, although the damage to our relationship had already been done. My pursuit put a tremendous amount of stress and strain on me and my Mom, and sadly, that manifested into anger. Despite my anger, my Mom, for whatever reason, didn't want to tell the truth about who I was ans where I came from. Perhaps she thought I was too young to learn my truth. Perhaps she didn't want to explain how I came to be their son. Shelbi always says, "Shame is a powerful drug. People get high off of it and it can, and often does, control their lives." Maybe that was why my Mother couldn't tell the whole truth. Shame. But what could she possible be ashamed of? What was she hiding? And why was she hiding it?

We stopped communicating all together. After years of questions and cryptic answers, we stopped talking. I lived my childhood and adolescence in a fog of mystery surrounding the identity of who I was. I didn't know where I came from, who my biological parents were, or how I came to my Mother and Father. When you're not raised with your biological family, and no one is giving you answers to these most pressing questions, you are left to fill in the blanks yourself. My self-talk led me to believe that I was unwanted, bad, unloved, and unworthy of love. For me, I had an even more fundamental question, "What am I?"

For better or for worse, my parents continued to distract me with shiny objects. They gave me whatever my heart desired, partly because they could, but also, because they were trying to distract me from those deeper questions that persisted in my mind. I knew I was being lied to and cajoled. I was a child, but I was smart. In hindsight, I wish she would have been honest with me. Knowing what I know now, and having experienced the pain and trauma of not knowing, has put me on a quest to help others learn their truth. I have discovered that the only way to live with abundance and joy is to be honest with yourself, those around you, and to God.

I can't remember much more about those years, however, the experiences I do remember left a lasting impression on me and my life. I'm not sure how many days or weeks, or perhaps months, had gone by, but soon after that first altercation on the playground with the Black kid, White kids started treating me bad too. I recall, one day, a White girl said, "I knew you were different; your eyes can't be blue. What are you?" Kids that were White stopped playing with me. I had made a pronouncement about being

Black and my skin, that defied that, caused more confusion and alienation. When I looked White and was considered White, I was OK with the White kids, but, when I said that I was Black in that altercation with the Black boy, my life got more difficult. I was rejected by my Black **AND** White friends. Not only am I dealing with Black kids teasing and rejecting me because I'm too White, but I was also dealing with White kids rejecting and separating from me, not wanting to be around me, because I said that I was Black. Here again, I was a child who was too White to be Black, and too Black to be White.

I remember telling my Momma that the other kids don't like me anymore because I'm neither Black nor White. All she said was, "People hated Jesus too and that is who you are to follow, Jesus. Be strong, lead by example, and learn now that it's lonely at the top." Her words fell on deaf ears, and I continued to defend myself in school and the neighborhood. I had countless fights that were most often sparked by a question related to my race, or my lack of knowledge thereof. The truth is that those comments hurt me deeply, and my hurt turned into anger, and my anger turned into rage. I enjoyed unleashing my rage on an unsuspecting bully who questioned my identity. I was no longer defending myself, rather, I was using their bodies as human punching bags to release the demons of fear and anger that resided in my soul. I fought so much that kids stopped teasing me. However, every change of school or change of environment started the anger cycle all over again. I had to train a new set of kids about my identity by fighting them, using my heavy hands and broken heart. I had to constantly prove my Blackness and defend myself from the hurtful comments. I had no retort, other than my fists.

I remember an incident when Momma and I went to a local store and a kid asked me, "Who is that lady?" I replied, "She's my Mom." He laughed and said, "Somebody's lying to you! She ain't your Mom." My Blackness has always been questioned, not only questioned, but outright rejected. Even in the most innocent environments, where I should have felt the safest. Who would claim me? My life was a real-life episode of the *Chapelle Show* where they had the race draft.

My anger and rage became my calling card. At

no time did my Mother address the root cause of it, rather, she decided to channel my energy but putting me in karate class. I was 6 turning 7. I think the idea was to keep me busy so I wouldn't ask her questions. I always had the best of everything, and karate class was no exception. I think that she was trying to overcompensate for whatever shame she was carrying related to my existence. I was not in just any ordinary karate class. My very first instructor was **the** Chuck Norris. That's right Chuck Norris. His approach to martial arts was meditative. He taught me to control my anger, and most importantly, to become self-disciplined. From ages 6 to 12, I was under his tutelage. I clearly remember his studio on Wilshire Boulevard, right down the street from McDonald's, a frequent stop after class.

Martial arts was vital to my survival growing up. By the time I was done training with Mr. Norris, I had learned not fight unless my life was in danger. I lived by the mantra, "Sticks and stones may break my bones but words can never hurt me." I stopped allowing words to trigger me, and I began to value myself, not matter what the outside world said. I soon discovered that the energy that I suppressed through martial arts would soon rear its ugly head.

Although my anger was under control, my energy was not, and Momma soon enrolled me in Pop Warner football. My coaches became members of my extended village, and my Mother welcomed as much help raising me as possible. She was really trying to give me a chance to be with more kids my color, so instead of me playing for all Black teams like Baldwin Hills, I played on Beverly Hills and Wilshire Athletic Club teams. The players on those teams *looked* like me. I loved everything about football -- the smell of the beautiful green grass, to the lifelong friends that were my teammates over the years. Football centered me, allowing me to gain more self confidence in my quest to identify who and what I was. In a strange way, I think all of my activities were there to serve me, and for me to learn more about myself. I was an exceptional football player, and by the time I reached my senior year of high school, I had over 50 letters from colleges to play. When it came to recruitment, I had a scarlet letter on my chest. I was lazy and rarely worked out in the gym. Many coaches said that I had too many distractions which caused the scouts to shy away from me as a prospect. Looking back, I was never supposed to progress beyond high school football. Though I loved the game and the fact that it helped me channel my aggression, if I would have gone further, I would never have been strong enough to look deeper at my life and discover who I was.

CHAPTER THREE

Let The Church Say Amen

Growing up, I was also very active in the church. I was an altar boy, sang in the choir, served as an usher, was active in Young People's Department, and participated in the Saturday Ethnic School Program. Indeed, my second home was Grant AME Church on 105th and Central.

Grant was a safe haven for me. Though it didn't offer answers to my ever-looming questions related to my own race or identity, it provided me a place to learn about Black people. Saturday Ethnic School was a repository of Black history. My Momma was doing her best to try to give me what she thought I needed, when all I ever wanted was my truth. In any event,

Saturday Ethnic School helped me find pride in my Blackness by learning about the pioneers of history like Harriet Tubman, Bishop Allen, founder of the AME Church, and Fredrick Douglass. I learned that I stood on bold, beautiful, Black shoulders and that I inherited the spirits of my ancestors and the strength that they possessed, despite not knowing who they were.

My love for Grant was beyond my weekly encounters at Ethnic School. I was really into church. I would pray, read the scripture, and serve during Sunday services. Many times, people would tell my Mother that I was going to be a preacher. Some members even started rumors that my biological Father was one of the bishops. "That boy is going to be a bishop like his Dad," they'd say. I laugh now, but then, they had no idea how painful their snide comments were. I didn't know if my parents *were* my parents and I had an inner turmoil that I lived with daily. I found myself constantly questioning my life and parentage, only to be teased by "saints of God." I was now having to deal with church rumors about who my real parents were, not to mention, Grant was, and remains, a predominantly Black church, and the church kids were also teasing me for being White. It seemed like I could never escape the constant ridicule, even at church.

Momma put plenty of activities in my life to try to distract me, and fill my mind with positivity. Keeping me busy and satisfied was her inoculation to the virus of lies that plagued my existence. Posing the question, "Are you my real Mother?" sent her into a frenzy, so I soon just resolved that I would never know the truth. At least, not from her. I stopped believing anything my Mother said. How could I not? Everything was either a lie or a distraction from the truth. If I can offer any advice on the subject, I would tell parents to please tell your children the truth. They know when you're lying, and it will only cause them emotional damage in the end. Telling the truth will save them from undue stress and unnecessary backlash. Shelbi told me that "The truth may not make you happy. The truth may not make you whole. But the truth will make you free." Tell your children the truth, they can handle it. Doing so will save them and you a lifetime of hurt and despair. My Mother did her best to try to mask what I needed by buying me things. She was compensating, not only for her inability to tell me the truth, but also for what happened with our family and my Father.

CHAPTER FOUR

My Father's Son

Children of divorce (or dissension) can struggle with identity. There really wasn't a time in my life when I saw my parents happily married. By my 7th birthday, Momma and my Dad were not living together. In fact, I only saw him on the weekends. I hated that. As a growing boy, I needed the daily presence of my Father, but, I suppose they had agreed to a different arrangement. I spent the weekdays with my Mother and Saturday, just Saturday, with my Father. I savored those Saturdays with him. Truth be told, I wish the tables had been turned and spent the week with my Dad and one day with Momma. I had her, but I needed him. My Father was so loving and tender, contrary to his immense frame that stood 6'5" and 550 pounds of Black man! He looked very intimidating, but to me, he was the calmest, most gentle man I've ever met.

I was never certain about what he did for a living, but I learned later that he was a very important man. He was an Army Veteran, but he never talked about his time in the service. I would love to have known where he had been stationed and what countries he went to, but he never spoke about it. I often wondered if he fought on the front lines or had exotic adventures. I imagined sitting at his feet listening to him tell tales of enemy combat and sweet victories, but those moments never happened. He wasn't the type to talk about the past.

I discovered that he was very high up in the Teamsters Union on the West Coast. From my understanding, he helped start the Union in California. He was known to have helped many workers and he fought for Black people to be admitted into the powerful organization. Instinctively, I knew that his high rank also made him a target. I am also aware of the nefarious conduct of some Union members, and my Father was not immune to that way of being. I recently learned that his initial introduction to the Union was quite unsavory. His role was carved out one night in 1938 when he was asked to "convince" another Union member to comply with a request made by the higher ups. A noble act, on the surface, however, in this instance, the "convincing" was enhanced with a baseball bat. He served a little less than 3 years in San Quintin, having been charged and convicted with assault with a deadly weapon and burglary. I didn't know any of that as a child, and I don't think it would have had a bearing on my admiration for my Father. All I knew then was that he was a superhero to me.

I remember when I was about 9 years old, my Dad and I were somewhere, and a man approached us. He reached out and hugged my Dad and said to me, "Your Dad is a Godsend. He saved me and my family and I could never repay him for all he did for me." I was shell shocked. I never learned what good deed my Father had done, but I was proud to be his son in that moment.

His personality was infectious, and he was a

good man. My Dad would help anyone. He even received awards for his service to the Union members. I remember dressing up in my tuxedo and bow tie to go to an awards ceremony in his honor. I used to have the plaque that he received, but choices that I made in my own life caused me to lose it, and most everything else that he once owned.

The great thing about him being high up in the Union was that he had many friends, from all walks of life. Some carried guns on their hips, and others raised cattle. Some were farmers, and others owned corporations. Each friend and associate that my Father had would often give him gifts. His friend that raised cattle would often gift us premium steak. As a child, when other kids were eating ground round, I would request and feast on a porterhouse, medium. No one ever thought there was anything strange about that. His farmer friends would send baskets or fresh fruits and vegetables that would accompany our over sized steaks. My Father was calm and measured. He rarely raised his voice at me, or anyone else. He affectionately called me "Dad" and when I would get beside myself, he would say calmly, "Don't be like that, Dad. God is not pleased with you." His approach was not to get the belt first, but to talk to me and find out why I acted out. His approach was decidedly different from my Mother's. He wasn't a churchgoer, but his countenance was more Christlike than the churchgoers at Grant.

My Father taught me how to be and how to respond, and not react. Jehovah's Witnesses would come to the door of my Mother's house and, like a lot of you, Momma would tell me to hide and not answer the door. It was like hide and seek. I really didn't know why we were not talking to these people. They looked nice and were dressed nice in suits and ties. Ladies would have on long dresses, and most of them would smile. I was always curious about what they wanted. They carried papers and books and I wondered what they said. But with Momma around, I would never know because we would hide like they had the plague or like they were armed gunman ready to attack. Almost daily, they would come to our house. They would knock a few times and Momma would say, "Shhhhhh." Then they would ring the doorbell and Momma would put her finger to her mouth to give me the hush sign. Then they would look in the window, but eventually, when no one answered, they would go away.

Daddy, on the other hand, embraced people. When the Jehovah's Witnesses knocked on his door, I would run and hide behind the couch because that is what I was taught by Momma. He would immediately usher me out from my hiding place. My Father welcomed them. He opened the door freely and invite them in. He often said that it's not nice to ignore people. He believed that our job was to be of service to people, including Jehovah's Witnesses. I was really confused. These were the same people that I hid from at my Mom's house. My Father would offer them a drink or a bowl of fruit, and we would have a wonderful conversation with the same people that I hid from the week before. We would chat for hours about their pamphlets and their beliefs. My Father was never rude or dismissive. He'd just listen, and I followed his lead.

Even with all the love my Dad gave me, he still wouldn't answer those most pressing questions -- where did I come from and how did you get me? He did his best to not dismiss my inquiry. He told me that, "Out of nowhere, your Mom brought you home one day." He explained that he wasn't my biological Father, but he WAS my Father. He told me, "You are my son, even if we didn't birth you." He went on to say, "Ask your Mom the details about how we got you." For some reason, I was OK with that answer from him.

Did I find out who my biological parents were then? No. Did I get answers to any of my questions? No. But I wasn't mad at him like I was with Momma. She never took the time to explain anything about me or how I came to be. Instead, she ignored me or yelled at me, or showered me with thing in hopes that I would stop asking. I was frustrated and angry with her for that. I would have much rather had her sit down and tell me the whole story, and I would never get it from her.

The confirmation that I got from my Father was calming. I finally had something to allay my sense of not belonging. I had a shred of information about my true identity, and I held on to that for years. That small bit of information mattered more to me than anything in the world. I had a Father who loved me, even though he wasn't my *Father*. This is why I kept his name. Our relationship continued to grow Saturday by Saturday. We would go somewhere every time I saw him. I realize now that my Mother was doing all the heavy lifting of parenting and my Father was having all the fun. He was the quintessential *Disneyland Dad*, literally and figuratively.

Our meetings weren't solely fun and games, though. My Father was a diabetic and I was charged with giving him his insulin shots when I was there. This hulking figure with a heart of gold would have to go into the hospital when his sugar levels dropped. I would lay awake praying every night, for him to return home and for God to make him well. Each time, God answered my prayer, and I would have my Dad back for another Saturday.

CHAPTER FIVE

The Women in My Life

For most of my life I've been surrounded by women. I was blessed to have strong, Godly women who played an intricate role in helping me throughout my life, even during the hard times. The Bible gives a clear example of how God provides exactly what you need when you need it. The ultimate test of Abraham's faith occurs when God tells him to sacrifice his only son, through whom he was to receive the promised blessing of becoming a great nation and through whom all the nations of the earth would be blessed, ultimately through Christ Jesus. Without hesitation, Abraham obeyed the Lord, and at the moment of his greatest sacrifice to God, "the Angel of the Lord called to him from heaven and said, "Do not lay your hand on the lad, or do anything to him, for now I know that you fear God, since you have not withheld your son, your only son, from Me." (Genesis 22: 11-12, NIV) "Then Abraham lifted his eyes and looked, and there behind him was a ram caught in a thicket by its horns. So, Abraham went and took the ram, and offered it up for a burnt offering instead of his son.

That story always resonated with me. There were days when I should have been on the chopping block, but my life was spared and a ram always appeared on my behalf. My first ram was my Godsister. After I was molested, I called into question my sexuality. In those days, "being soft" was a cardinal sin. My tendencies were effeminate and I was changing every day. I remember receiving backlash for my "girlish" ways, but no one ever asked me why I had a shift. They were only concerned with the outcome, but never addressed the root cause of my changing behavior. For Halloween, my Momma would dress me up as a lady, complete with a dress, high heels, make up and a wig. I would switch, put my hands on my hips. I would speak with a high pitched voice and flip my hair when people spoke to me. The act itself was innocent, but the reasoning behind my comfort was more sinister. By no means do I believe that behavior determines sexuality, on the contrary. What I do know is that no one ever considered that my sexual innocence was tampered with and that I was acting out in a way that was counter to my feelings.

I started to believe that because I had won the contest dressed as a woman and that I my Mother had gay friends, coupled with my body responding after the molestation, that I must be gay. I didn't have any more information than that. My 7 year-old mind was searching for identity and I landed on being a gay male because that is what made sense to me at the time. All of the pieces fit together, and no one ever asked me or talked to me about my decision. I now know that sexuality isn't determined by wearing a Halloween costume or by being molested. People can't behave their way gay or straight. You are who you are, how you were created. My grown man self knows that, but my child self had no clue. Not only did I not know, but many in my life didn't know how to articulate those things either.

My Godsister, Connie, is a very strong-willed person. She's tough. She was would always tell me the truth. She helped me to understand my true being. I wasn't soft and I wasn't gay. She really helped me put my life back on track, event though I never told her what happened to me. My Godfamily helped me escape, just for a little while, the turmoil that I was dealing with at Momma's house. I was no longer confused. I learned that things happen in life and it's up to me to decide how it affects me. I have lived by that mantra for my whole life, and it has served me well.

My time at my Godfamily's house was a welcomed departure from my real life at home. I would go over to their house on the Fourth of July and eat BBQ, pop fireworks, play basketball, go to the park around the corner, and play games. Although they loved me and welcomed me into their home and family, they still could not or would not answer any of my questions about who I really was. At this point in my life, I was still seeking out information about my identity from everyone I knew. I had become a master of appearing fine on the outside, but every minute of every hour I was consumed with the question of who I was. No one was safe. I asked everyone I knew, two and three times. Everything I thought to be true was a lie, and my emotional cracks were beginning to splinter and show. I was ignored and avoided and all I wanted was the truth.

Another ram in my life was my "sister" GG. She has been a stable force in my life and one of the sweetest ladies I've ever known. Most significantly, she helped me understand that Momma beat everybody. She took the excuse away that Momma treated me differently because I was not biologically hers. I thought for so long that my Mother hated me because I didn't live up to what she imagined or desired in a son. GG helped me understand that my Mother treated me the way that she did because of own issues, not because she didn't birth me. This was vital to me. Knowing that I was treated like everyone else freed me from the bonds of feeling alienated and different. I didn't want to be singled out or treated unfairly. I believe everyone should be treated with compassion and kindness. There is a common denominator in all cultures, and it is love. I expected my Mother to be loving and compassionate toward me, but I soon realized that I was holding her to a standard that I didn't hold myself to. GG looked at my Mother through God's eyes and was not critical of her or the situation. She taught me to operate with grace when I dealt with my Mother and to remember that just like I had a story, my Mother did too.

Although my cousin GG offered me guidance and direction with her sweet disposition, she also could not answer my questions. I was growing into my manhood and I gained a tremendous amount of wisdom, but I wanted more. I wanted someone, anyone, to tell me my story. My intention for having these women in my life was to get closer to answer my most burning questions. I was living, but not knowing who I was or where I came from, continued to burden my soul and weigh on my heart.

My Aunt Becky entered my life and she helped me to see my own greatness, not to mention, she would often go toe-to-toe with Mother. She was a realist who didn't have time to coddle my Mother or excuse her conduct. She gave it her straight, no chaser. The only thing that would deter her from offering unsolicited advice or checking my Mother because of her deplorable behavior, was *All My Children. All My Children* was her show!

Aunt Becky had several grandkids, some biological, some not. It didn't matter to her. I was never an outcast or an afterthought when I was with Aunt Becky. I was family. She taught me to speak my mind, and to fight for what I wanted. She constantly assured me that I was loved by my Mother. My ears heard her, but it took my heart years to catch up.

We would sit at her kitchen table and feast on the best pigs feet and neck bones, talking about everything under the sun. Though Aunt Becky was a good cook, my Momma was a caterer for movie stars, because she could cook her butt off. Monkey Bread, the buttery kind, pies, greens, biscuits and gravy, milk gravy, and fried chicken to die for. Gumbo, chilled shrimp, fried shrimp, mac and cheese, roast, brown gravy, soups, and casseroles. She fed my belly, but my soul was starving.

I watched Momma cook every day. She wouldn't let me in the kitchen at first, but after she worked her culinary magic, I was charged with washing dishes and taking out the trash. I was 7. My tiny frame couldn't reach the sink, so I had a step stool to help me reach the faucet. Slowly, but surely Momma started letting me do prep work on the food. I started off by washing vegetables, and when she trusted me enough to use a knife, I would dice just like she wanted. I mimicked her stance in the kitchen -- one hand on a spoon or pot, the other on my hip.

On occasion, we abandoned our cooking duties and went out to eat. My Mother believed in fine dining. We frequented Lawry's for prime rib and The New Moon for Asian cuisine. Over dinner one evening, I asked her yet again about my identity and where I came from. I got no response. She was actively ignoring me and keeping my story a secret. I was frustrated and decided that I would pose the question again to Aunt Becky. I asked. She told me that she didn't know where I came from. She offered a little bit of information. She told me that one day my Momma just brought me home and she was concerned. She asked my Mother where she got "the white baby" from. My Mother offered no information, and Aunt Becky didn't press the issue. How do you just <u>not</u> have a child one day, but then have one the next, and no one thinks that's strange? I was even more confused. She went on to say that she thought that my Aunt Sayran had been with my Mother when she got me. I had known my Aunt Sayran my entire life. She was my Mother's dear friend, and I think that her name was actually Sarah, but as a child, I named her Sayran. We weren't related, but in Black culture, children never addressed an adult by just their first name, and often, names were simple created. To me she was, and will always be Aunt Sayran.

I didn't have much contact with Aunt Sayran because she lived in Las Vegas. I rarely saw her and never had an opportunity to ask her any questions when I was a child. I tucked that tidbit away in my heart until I was old enough to pull it out and ask her. I knew that in order to get answers, I had to talk to Aunt Sayran. And I did, 30 years later.

My quest for information wasn't over. I took every opportunity to ask everyone in my life if they knew who I was and where I came from. Folks would only say that one day your Momma just showed up with this little white baby boy. It was helpful, to a degree, but I had no concept of what that meant. It was helpful because I had a start. People who have no knowledge of their biological family often feel like they just fell from the sky. Their beginnings are steeped in mystery, and they find themselves making up wild stories to center themselves in the belief that they had a beginning. Saying I showed up as a baby reminded me that I had been a baby. Someone gave birth to me and cared for me. I had a start. The people around me knew something. I was the only person in the dark. They kept the secret and made the decision to never tell me. Because they all knew my story, they treated me special, with kid gloves. Most people felt sorry for me and offered me subtle sympathy.

Despite my challenges and the feelings of abandonment, I really enjoyed my childhood. When you don't have the truth, your mind can, in its own way, protect you from pain and despair. My thoughts, then, were all over the place. It reminds me of the song, "My Minds Playing Tricks On Me," by the Geto Boys. My mind, was indeed, a tricky place. It confused me to the point where my thoughts were constantly seeking balance between fantasy and reality.

No matter how frustrated I became, there were still more people trying to make a difference in my life. My Aunt Gerry Smith was another woman in my life who rescued me from the fortress of my mind. She was a heavy-handed lady who played no games. She ruled, much like my Momma, with a Bible in one hand and a belt in the other.

For the first 6 years of my life, my Aunt Gerry taught me discipline and freedom from the burden of my mystery. She exposed me to the arts, and I loved to sing for her. I was a member of the the Little Angels Choir that she directed at First AME Church in Los Angeles. The arts were my source of freedom. I was able to be me and explore new feelings and new experiences. She told me many times that there is a time to play and a time to be serious. I wish I would have listened to her a little earlier in my childhood. She once told me, "Your Mom really does love you because she adopted you." At some point I started to become numb to the fact that my Mom loved me. I focused more on the fact she had evidence about me and wouldn't tell me the truth. Her love was inconsequential, because I just wanted to know my truth. Aunt Gerry, like all the rest, had no information about me either. I was lost, and yet found.

My Aunt Viv was my partner. I loved her too. Her full name was Vivian Rice and she was an usher at Second AME Church in Los Angeles. She took me to all of the Los Angeles Rams home games because she had season tickets. We would leave church and head to the Coliseum and watch the Rams play. Her influence and her love of sports inspired me to play and because of those Sundays wearing my blue and gold, I'm still a Rams fan to this day. When the Olympics came to L.A. in 1984, she took me watch basketball, judo, swimming, and wrestling competitions. It was always fun to be with her. She had a calm demeanor, but like all of the other women in my life, she was very strict.

My Aunt Viv had no idea where I came from, who my biological parents were, or the circumstances surrounding my adoption. She would say, "You'll find them one day." This hope was a motivator for me, giving me something to look forward to. I still wondered and felt like everyone knew something that I didn't. It was like walking into a room when people are speaking a foreign language. They all know what's being said, but I was trying to decipher clues and innuendo to find my truth. Why wouldn't some one, any one, talk to me and tell me the truth? All of these people claimed to love me, yet everyone was lying to me.

CHAPTER SIX
Double Digits

By the time I was 10 years-old, my desire to know my story was ever present in my mind. The constant teasing from my peers was routine and predictable. My family made further attempts at distracting me from the hunger of my truth with sports. I was a great football player, and a pretty good basketball player too. I had friends, played the trumpet, and sang in choirs all over Los Angeles. Daddy Bill was still in my life and by now, he was my world. He was the only person that I trusted, the one who understood me. He was my Dad, but he was also my friend. He listened to me and he tried his best to give me most of what I wanted, and everything I needed.

One day at school I was enduring the routine heckling about my skin color from a boy in my class. His words were harsh, and they triggered my fight response. We made plans to fight later that day. We squared up that afternoon. I swung first and connected my right fist to his jaw. A loud crack echoed and I threw a barrage of punches to his face and body. He stumbled, then swung back. Before I knew it, we were in a full brawl. While we were fighting, I was all over him kicking his ass. I was screaming, "WHAT YOU CALL ME? IMMA BEAT YOUR ASS". I landed blow after blow and was blinded with rage. Mid swing, I noticed that my Dad's best friend had driven up. He always carried a gun and he served as my Father's bodyguard as well as his driver. He rushed over toward me and in one single swoop, pulled me off of the kid that I was wailing on. Still flailing, I was heaved into his long, light blue, convertible Cadillac. I rested my out of breathe body on the white leather seats.

"Where are we going?" I asked between rapid breaths. "I was about to kill that kid!"

He responded calmly, "To your house. Your Mom has something to tell you."

I was curious, but not concerned. Although this had never happened, I was too busy basking in the glow of my victory over that kid to worry about it. What could she possibly want to tell me? As we wound through the streets of L.A., my spirit got quiet. That car ride seemed like it took forever, even though we were right down the street.

We got to the house and my Mother met us at the door, in tears. She grabbed me and squeezed me hard. She bent down over my 10 year-old body and said, "Bill's gone. "He's gone baby". My entire world crumbled in that moment. My only coping mechanism was to fight, so I started hitting and punching Daddy Bill's friend who had the gun. I went ballistic. All he could do was hug me. I think I blacked out after that because I don't remember anything except the funeral that occurred several days later. I lost my hero that day. The day that I fought a kid for calling me names, my Father was dying. My young mind felt tremendous guilt and shame. While my Father was spending the last moments of his life fighting to breathe, I was shaming myself, him, and my family fighting because someone said a cross word about me. I felt terrible. He was gone and I had shamed the family name. My young mind couldn't process it all.

My Dad hated when I fought. He taught me that sticks, and stone may break my bones, but names should never hurt me. He preached that to me. "Dad," he would say, "you have to learn to control your temper."

For a long time, I believed that it was my fault that my Daddy was dead. If I wasn't fighting, he would still be here. I thought that God was punishing me. This inner pain followed me for decades, wreaking havoc in my life, and adding more reasons to a growing list of why I don't love or value myself. I'm 10, I don't know who I am. I've been molested. At school, I am harassed and teased every single day about my race and skin color. My family is broken and everyone who says that they love me aren't telling me the truth. Now, the most important person on the planet to me, is gone and I've killed him.

As a kid, I didn't know that my Dad died from a heart attack due to his weight and diabetes. No one told me. I believed that his death was my fault. I had no one to talk to and I didn't know how to feel. How was I supposed to feel? On the day of his funeral the mood was understandably sad and solemn. The church was full to capacity and in the front, high and lifted up, was a gold casket. My Father, even in death, had the best of everything. The organ music started, and people began walking up to see my Dad's lifeless body. I waited my turn to see my Daddy. I wanted to see him. I needed to see him. The wait took forever. One-by-one, person after person paid their respects to my Dad. I was standing on the seat trying to get a glance, but with the throngs of mourners around his casket, I couldn't see him. Finally, it was time for the family to view my Dad. As I hopped down from the pew and readied myself to walk past his body, I was stopped in my tracks. I'm not sure who it was, but they forbade me from seeing him. They refused to let me go. He was **MY** Dad! My fight response was triggered, once again, and I started kicking and fighting anyone in my path. I wanted to see my Daddy and they wouldn't let me. I was inconsolable. "Why? Why can't I go see my Daddy?," I wailed. My Father's body guard swooped me up and took me outside. I kept asking him why? Why? He just held me like he did that day I was told that my Dad was gone.

I never forgot that moment. It is etched in my mind and has scarred me for life. I never got closure and that moment would revisit me in my dreams for years. I was mad at everyone who held me back. If you ever find yourself in this position, I advise you to never do this to a child. It will harm them forever. If that child wants to go up and see the casket of their parent, let them. It's a better alternative than what I experienced. All I could see as they dragged me out of the chapel was this big, beautiful gold box. I never got to say goodbye and I never forgot that feeling.

After his funeral, I cried for days. Even now, after everything I've been through, that is still the worst day of my life. I lost my leader, my teacher, my psychiatrist, my Father, and my friend. William "Bill" Williams. I loved him then and I love him now and I thank him for all that he did for me. Part of me rests in that gold box with my Dad, and I pray that I have been able to make him proud. My road, after his death was rough, but I have landed on my feet. Though they are scrapped and scarred, I am Daddy Bill's son, and for that reason alone, I win the fight every time.

76

CHAPTER SEVEN

Dying is easy. Living is harder.

After any death, the hardest thing to do is live. We, who are left behind, have the cruel job of living life without those we've loved and lost. It's awful. When my Dad died, I thought my life was over. I was more lost than I had ever been. Now, as an older man, I've come to know that when we lose someone we love, they continue to live on through us. I tell my kids all the time how wonderful Daddy Bill was. He was a loving and peaceful man. I do my best to live, everyday, as close to his earthly example and Jesus' heavenly one. It's a decision and a calculated effort to do it daily. As a Father, Daddy Bill gave me a very high bar to strive for and I'm grateful for it, even if, on occasion, I fall short of its reach.

As I entered my early teens, I became more difficult to deal with. My Mother didn't know how to handle me, and I blamed her for my rage and anger. She represented everything I didn't understand or like about myself, and now, my most valuable jewel was in a gold box. I blamed her. She was frustrated too. Her method of controlling my explosive behavior was to beat me. Non-corporal discipline had stopped working, and I was no longer responding to her. Grounding me also wasn't a threat. I had become an introvert and I enjoyed being alone. I didn't mind those punishments that included isolation from the rest of the world. I would sit in my room after she punished me, and simmer like a pot, just waiting to explode. My Mother could take everything away from me, and I was completely unphased. I didn't care. I still had to go to church 4 times a week though. I still had football practice on Mondays, Wednesdays, and Fridays, and a weekly game on Saturdays. Momma never took away from football, karate, or church. Beating me was her best and, at that point, only option, when, until I was about 12 years-old when I became immune to those too.

Iris was a family friend. After my Father died, she would spend time with Momma and me from time to time. She was an executive for a major computer company. She would glide in and out of our lives like a breeze. She also witnessed the way Momma dealt with me. She would often come and get me and take me out, just so that I could find escape from the chaos. We would hang out all over Los Angeles. Sometimes, we would just sit her car and listen to music or got to a movie. Her job required that she go out of the country on occasion. When she was gone, I was miserable. Her returns to California were salve to my wounded heart. She saved me from the tension and violence that plagued our home and the soul of my Mother. Iris also gave me the courage to stand up to Momma and ask for the truth. Iris would remind me that I had the right to know who my *real* parents were. I agreed. I did have the right and I needed the answers.

My cousins, Yaya and Wubby would often pick me up and take me anywhere I wanted to go. I was in desperate need of an outlet, any outlet, that would keep my mind occupied. When I was idle, I became internally destructive, and that was a dangerous mental space. I remember them taking me to Cal Poly Pomona to watch a basketball game. They were cheerleaders, so I got preferential seating and treatment. I had so much fun. I was able to just enjoy the game and not think about the life that awaited me at home. Yaya remains a steady rock for me and, I think, in her own way, even then, she saw my pain and wanted to help me. Her love has been a constant vibration in my heart and, in those moments that I didn't feel loved, or believe that I deserved love, I would rest in knowing that Yaya love me.

When I was 17, I gathered up all the courage that I had in my body, and boldly posed the question to my Mother. I approached her and told her that I had a right to know who I was. My request wasn't just a question from a son to a Mother, it was a desperate plea from a young man who was lost to the only person who had the keys to unlock the mysteries of my life . I was slowly dying inside. I had already lived through some difficult seasons in my short life, and I was at my wits end. She was my only hope. She listened quietly as I made my plea. When I was done and my heart was racing out of my chest, my Mother looked me in the eye and said that she didn't know anything about me or where I came from. I was stunned. Even then, as I stood hopeless and shallow, she didn't tell me anything. I knew that she had more information to share, but she refused. I called her a liar. We yelled back and forth a full hour. I was not giving up. I asked for my adoption paperwork, and she refused to give those to me too. I wanted to know. Then, in the heat of the moment, she blurts out, "Your real Father is in jail." I stopped mid-scream and stumble backward as if a ball of energy had hit me squarely in my frontal lobe. My mind got foggy, and I was stunned. "What!!!!" I yelled. "You liar! He's not in jail!" I stormed out of the room in a haze of rage and confusion. Jail? My Father? Jail? I had no clue what to do with that information. My mind went blank and everything that I thought I knew about my life and my world was immediately in question. I was in a full-fledged identity crisis, and no one cared enough to help me.

My subconscious was doing a number on me. I

began to question her motivation and why she told me about my biological Father in that way. I thought, *after all these years now she wants to tell me this? She just wants me to think he is unavailable, so I won't ask about him anymore. He's not in jail.* That's what happens when secrets are kept. Everyone in the situation is operating with the belief that life is OK, when in fact, life is swirling out of control, on a path to sure destruction. Lies and deceptions are the cornerstone of crisis. That's what was happening in that moment. I was in crisis because her inattention to my request earlier on spawned another Cancer in my family. I didn't trust anything that she said at this point. I didn't know her heart or her intentions and I was angrier than ever before.

I was also experiencing a tremendous about of guilt for yelling and berating my Mother. My faith had taught me to honor my Mother and Father, and I wasn't doing that at all. My wounded soul was too damaged to honor her. I was in the church all my life and was even preaching, but I was living on the fence. One foot in the church because I knew that's where I belonged, and one foot out of the church because I was living with this inner anger. Because of my earlier exposure to sexual acts, I had adopted an unhealthy sex drive that was hindering my spiritual growth. I couldn't control my anger, my temper, or my raging sexual urges. My rage was being unleashed on my Mother, whom I loved, and my sex drive was wreaking havoc in my soul. I decided that physical pleasure was enough to mask my feelings of shame and anger, and my increasing promiscuity was my way of coping. I became a womanizer. I'm sure I was trying to overcompensate for my childhood abuse, so I tried to kiss and have sex with every girl I could.

My life started taking a turn in the wrong direction. I stopped listening to people and started rationalizing the Bible to fit my own agenda. I used the Bible to justify my sinful behavior. My word of caution to all is, never ever use God's word to make your sin OK, or use your sin to cause someone else to sin. You will psy dearly, trust me.

The guilt of living with my behavior haunted me. I was sorry for what I did to all those sweet girls. Playing with their feelings and emotions was wrong and I regret every encounter. If you are one of those young women I hurt, please forgive me. I was a teenager who had not yet learned how to love. I know I can't go back and change or fix my actions, I can at least acknowledge my mannish, inappropriate behavior and apologize for it.

At the time, I didn't see what I was doing as sin. I had learned about sin, but that term, to me described murderers and thieves. I was exempt from the wrath of God because I was a teenager who was *only* having sex with multiple girls and disrespecting my Mother at every turn. I figured that since I was young, my sins wouldn't carry long-lasting weight and life-long consequences. I knew that Jesus died on the cross for our sins, so if He had already died, I might as well sin and enjoy the spoils before real punishment came. I'd ask for forgiveness later. In her calm soft voice, Rochel, a friend and spiritual sounding board for me, would do her best to explain why I was wrong, and that true repentance means turning completely away from sin, never doing that offense again. Hebrews chapter 10 verses 26-31 covers this truth. We would talk on the phone forever. Our conversations would last for hours and I loved talking to her.

Eventually, she would have to say, "Bye Billy I gotta go to bed get off my phone." After hanging up, I would sit quietly processing all that she said.

I wish I would have listened to her much sooner. Rochel did her best to give me the truth, but I was not willing to apply it to my life yet. Had I listened, I would have avoided the grave consequences that I dealt with because of my sinful behavior. I wasted a lot of time and spent many nights lonely and distraught.

Although Rochel was wise, she had no idea where I came from, how I arrived, or the identity of my biological parents. She heard the same rumors as everyone else. She really tried to make it seem like that those rumors weren't that important. More than that, she comforted me on the subject all the time doing whatever she could to make me understand no matter where I came from, I was supposed to follow God and live according to His Will.

My high school math teacher, Ms. Lane, was a force of nature. She taught at my beloved alma mater, Crenshaw High School. Ms. Lane wasn't in my life long -- only for 3 years. She taught me algebra, geometry, and trigonometry. I passed her class, all three years. I remember getting a C or F on a test and Ms. Lane called me in the classroom when everyone was gone. She told me about myself in her calm voice. She stressed to me the importance of my education, and that even though she knew I was a football player, that sports weren't everything. More than anything, Ms. Lane taught me how to be more serious about life. She would tell me to stop playing around and think about my life. She explained to me that life is a serious matter, and I had to treat it as such. Her influence sobered me in a time when I felt out of control. My spirit life was in turmoil, and my mind was still consumed with finding out who I came from.

CHAPTER EIGHT

Shades of Gray

By the time I graduated from high school, I had grown
to understand that I was different. Not just because I
didn't know who my biological parents were, but each
time I looked into a mirror, I saw a White man staring
back at me. My skin was White, but my soul was
Black. It sounds foolish to say, but that is my truth. I
had bought in to the notion that skin color determines
identity when I was fighting in kindergarten, but now,
as a young adult, I was challenged with the reality that
the world either respond to my skin or they would see
my heart. I had learned about the atrocities placed
upon Black people by White people. White privilege,
though not a term that I knew then, was seen in every

facet of my life. White kids had parents that bought them brand new cars that they didn't have to work for. They had credit cards so they could shop anytime and anywhere. White people mistreated Black folks. I was a Black man, trapped in White skin and the world never considered that I was a shade of gray. I didn't know what I should be beholden to, so I decided to be beholden to myself, not the Whiteness of my skin or the Blackness of my soul. I would no longer feel this urgency to pick one race that I should be or to live by. I was exhausted trying to determine what culture I should follow and become.

After growing up Black, there is no way I could ever define myself as a White person because of the hurt inflicted on Black people by them. Their savage acts could not be a part of my history, and I had no intention of making their story part of my story. But my skin defied my intention. My hue prevented me from being my full Black self and the world reminded me that I had to be one or the other.

People want to know where White people get this privileged attitude. I will tell you! It's from not having consequences to the White man's in-humane treatment of every other race, color, and creed, and I certainly didn't want to have a place in that savagery. There is nothing in America that the White man has obtained that was not stolen. I knew this to be true then, and I know this to be true now. I did not want any parts of it. If you say I'm White, I'll respond like I did at the rodeo, "I ain't White, I'm Black!"

Many people see my White skin and wonder why I would elect to live my life as a Black man when it would be so easy for me to "pass." After all, it is difficult to be a Black man in this country. My answer is simple; I'd rather push through the adversities of life in a fair way, than to take advantage of people, hurt communities, and steal from families just to get ahead.

This behavior is what I continue to see from the White community and no one from their race is stepping up to do or say anything about it. Instead, Whites are taking away voting rights and making it harder for people of color to vote. They often make excuses for their behavior, using God as their reference. Why would I want to be a part of that type of people? I could have easily passed for White, but kindergarten taught me well — people's opinions of you are their problem, not yours. Had I chosen to "pass" they would have rejected me anyway.

> After Daddy Bill died, Momma tried her best to put good Black men in my life. Gil was one of them. I'm not sure how he came in my life or where Momma knew him from, but he was a great man. Gil would take me fishing at Castaic Lake on a regular basis. It was so beautiful. I learned to love the outdoors. Seeing the sun glisten on the lake top was a site to see. Gil taught me how to bait a hook, tie the hook to the fishing line, and cast. Almost everything about fishing I learned from Gil. We would make sandwiches and fill a cooler full of drinks, get up while it was still dark, and get on that freeway headed to the lake. Most of the time I couldn't sleep the night before because I was nervous with anticipation for the trip. Gil told me the reason we were able to go fishing all the time was because he had worked hard and "put his time in." He said the Bible teaches that a man must work to eat. Gil had worked hard and retired from a government job and received a nice steady pension. This was why we could enjoy ourselves, because he worked long and hard, so we could play and relax. I

loved that man, but when I left California, I never heard from him again and always wondered what happened to him.

Paul Kidd, Jr. was another significant male influence in my life. He was a well-known radio DJ on 1580 KDAY. He had a great gospel show on Sunday mornings in L.A. I loved his show and listened to it weekly. Along with his radio gig, Paul was a grill master. He made a BBQ sauce called Touch of Soul BBQ Sauce. He always talked to me about making something of my life, stressing the importance of having a job or, ideally, owning your own business. He started me on an entrepreneurial journey by hiring me to deliver his BBQ sauce to waiting customers.

We would go to the plant where they were making the sauce. It was so cool to see bottles going around the machine being filled with his signature BBQ sauce. I would watch as it was boxed and loaded into delivery trucks, ready to be delivered all over California. This was my first real job. I loved Paul Kidd and I believe he really loved me. The time that I spent with him was a welcomed distraction from the constant nagging question of my identity. He normalized my life and never made me feel different. I was accepted and loved, just because.

I was developing into the fullness of my manhood and my Mother recognized those changes. With the help of all of the Father figures that she invited into my life after my Dad died, I was beginning to see the totality of my life as a Black man. The time came for me to begin getting serious about how I wanted to live and what I wanted. My Uncle Martin and my Mom began preparing me to take over the mortuary that he owned.

Uncle Martin was very successful Black man that owned a funeral home. As a mortician, you would expect that he would be a bit creepy. The truth is that he was a very cool guy with a creepy job! Late one night, I was awakened by Momma. She told me that we had to go with Uncle Martin because somebody had broken into the mortuary. I rubbed my burning eyes and slipped on my robe and slippers. We went into the mortuary through the back door, because no one knew if the perpetrator was still inside. In those days, drug addicts would break into mortuaries to steal embalming fluid to make sherm, a potent hallucinogenic drug.

We followed Uncle Martin in. The back door was open. I slowly walk towards the door and saw rows of metal tables lined up, end to end. My heart was pounding. I turned to my left and got a glimpse of a naked female body. It was gray and stiff. I think I was in shock because I couldn't take my eyes off of that body. I had never seen a dead person before, and I began wondering if my Father was that stiff and gray as he laid in that gold coffin. Fear gripped me as I slowly backed out of the room with my eyes fixed on that body.

I had visited the mortuary many times before, but I had always used the front entrance. From the time that I was around 11, I worked services there. I would be in charge of handing out programs and directing people to the viewing rooms. I cleaned and vacuumed all the room and the little chapel where my Uncle would hold funerals. I never thought the work was morbid until I saw that body in the back room. Uncle Martin taught me the importance of honest work. He also taught me the art of dressing like a gentleman. He was sharp as a razor. He was the epitome of class and sophistication without being trite or trendy. He was a man's man, and I've followed that example my entire life.

As accomplished and sophisticated as he was, my Uncle Martin also had the daunting task of dealing with my attitude in my teens. He did his best to keep me straight. When I talked back, he would give that stern stare that reminded me that he was in control. He told me on several occasions that I had to stop being silly and to "grow up." My way of being was combative and annoying. One time, Uncle Martin left the house and was gone for weeks. I asked Momma where he was, and she said that I hurt his feelings so bad he had to stay away for a while. I didn't understand what was happening. Here I was, yet again, feeling worthless and responsible for the loss of another man that was in my life. Momma's anger was fueled by my blunt approach. I told the truth. I had told Uncle Martin, in a fit of anger, that he wasn't my daddy. As soon as the words left my mouth, I regretted them ever forming. I compounded my mistake by then asking Uncle Martin if he knew the identity of my biological family. I probably shouldn't have said, "you're not my Dad" but, he and Momma were not married so he wasn't my Father by marriage or biologically. I never considered that his feelings would be hurt. What's funny is that he was as close to me as any good father is to his son. He did the things a Father does. I was selfish and single-minded as a young man. Uncle Martin couldn't tell me who my parents were, so I didn't really care how he felt. I know this sounds bad, but it's the truth. I let not knowing who my parents were affect who and how I treated the great people that I had present in my life. I let my anger and shame of not knowing who I was go so far, that I hurt people I really cared about.

Uncle Martin reemerged into my life, and we made up for lost time. We worked in the garden together growing onions, tomatoes, peppers, and greens. I will always remember how good, how sharp, how dedicated a man Uncle Martin was, even though I wasn't as good to him as he was to me.

I was 16 years old, and Uncle Martin had continued to be a stabilizing force in my life. We had the most profound conversations, but I still didn't know who my parents were and, although he gave me so much, the one thing that I needed most, he could not provide. In fact, nobody was willing to help me. I was upset. I acted out. I needed answers. I deserved answers.

During those days, people thought it was OK to ignore my questions and to negate my feelings. They dodged them like a speeding car aiming for their knees, jumping out of the way of my persistence just in the nick of time. It was difficult for me to remain silent and to pretend that it wasn't killing me inside. Most adoptees, or rather, those of unknown parentage, feel the same way. We walk among the masses of "normal" people who know who they come from, but are forced to remain quiet and just accept life as it comes. That was what I did for decades. It's a ridiculous notion to assume a person, being ignored, wouldn't eventually explode at some point. Not knowing who my blood family was, made me start to think that people were appeasing me and giving me things just to shut me up. They were all trying to buy my silence. It never worked for me. No matter how well I did in life, no matter my accomplishments, no matter the people I already had in my life loving me, not knowing my roots was a hole in my soul that no material possession or adventurous experience could fill.

After a while, the void caused me to become stripped of compassion. I felt lost. I felt all alone. I felt incomplete. I didn't feel part of anybody or anything, and I started losing trust in people. All the lies being told over this vast world contributed to the destruction of my well-being, and it took my faith, my trust, and almost, my life.

I was keenly aware that I was being lied to. Most people like me know they are being lied to, too. We will seek any and everything to help us to feel whole. For me, I was on a quest for answers that seemed like the magic bullet to my aching need for wholeness. Around the same time, while my world was turning upside down, I rediscovered something that changed, and should have saved my life. Football.

CHAPTER NINE

Offsides

I spent a great deal of my time on the football field at Crenshaw High School. I needed an outlet and, given my frame, and natural propensity for aggression, football suited me. Football allowed me to express my rage and do so without significant consequence. My coaches loved my "passion for the game." What they didn't know was I was working out my emotional turmoil on the heads of our opponents. With every snap of the ball, I sunk deeper into the darkness of a secret that was held in the hearts and minds of those who purported to care for me. I fell in love with football, but, just as with any love, another, more intoxicating draw beckoned me.

She came in the form of a white powdery substance that guaranteed, from my first hit, to take away my pain and rage. She was faithful, and did just that. I was enamored with cocaine and her sly way of lulling me into a false sense of joy and tranquility. What I didn't realize was that cocaine is a jealous mistress and she demands complete loyalty.

By the time I reached my senior year in high school, I was working out my rage on the field, and nurturing my pain one hit of cocaine at a time. Cocaine hurt me dearly in my teens. I had received several full scholarship offers to play football in college, but because of my addiction and my reluctance to get help, they faded like mist. I lost them all. The letters and the calls stopped, and the courting by coaches that once bubbled like a gumbo pot, cooled to a slow simmer, and then ran cold. Rumors got out about me and my drug usage, and all the scouts fled. Even with the heartbreak of losing my shot at a college, and perhaps a professional football career, God still provided a ram in the bush.

My great friend, and brother from another Mother, Henry Anderson told me to talk to his Father about going away to school. He had been a proponent for Black kids to go to historically Black colleges and universities (HBCUs). Henry's Father was a doctor who graduated from Cheyney University. Cheyney is a small Black college located in Pennsylvania. A portion of Cheyney's campus served as a historic route line for the Underground Railroad. At the time of Dr. Anderson's urging that I attend Cheyney, I was still busy doing cocaine and thinking very little about my future. I didn't realize how important the opportunity was, so I continued my path of destruction. Although I was a great football player, had been named captain of the team as a freshman, and had been nominated for football honors, I chose the thing that would satisfy me, making my pain go away. Instead of becoming a college student, I became a full-fledge cocaine addict.

By grace, I was allowed to attend Cheyney anyway. When I arrived on to Cheyney's campus, I dreamt of graduating, and then being in NFL Draft. My dream was to play for the Philadelphia Eagles, but cocaine, like I said, was a jealous lover. On a whim, Coach Buddy Ryan came out to Cheyney to work out our senior safety. He gave me a lot of attention and told me I had what it took to make it in the NFL. He told me that all I had to do was work hard, and I could have a real shot. My dream as a kid was to play in the NFL, and I smoked and snorted it away. There was no one to blame but myself for succumbing to drugs and undisciplined behavior. In true addict form, I quickly found a dealer when I arrived in Pennslyvania. Addicts call dealers "plugs." I found one and started using cocaine more heavily. I stopped going to class and did so poorly, that I lost my privilege to play on the team. As an athlete, you must maintain an "C" average to suit up. I didn't have that. My grades fell to 4 Fs and 2 Ds. I was unceremoniously booted from the team and lost all rights, privileges, and benefits that go along with playing college football.

Not only did I let Dr. Anderson down, but I also let myself, and my Dad down. That was the worst pain. I had shamed myself and his name with my conduct. At this point in my life, I felt like I couldn't do anything right. I was supposed to be this preacher born from a bishop. I was not. I was supposed to be a football player headed to the NFL. I was not. I was just a lonely, rejected young man losing all grips on life. I grew angrier and angrier, and I still didn't know who I was. I was a lost soul. The crazy thing is that as my life was spinning out of control, I knew I had the power and resources to hit the brakes and change direction. I slowly drifted away from family. I felt incomplete and I was dying inside.

On top of everything, my Mother was disgusted by my behavior. I dropped out of school, stopped singing in choirs, and stopped my ministry training. Momma Carrie had had enough. After I returned home from Cheyney my freshman year, she kicked me out and sent me to her brother's house to live. As I was packing up to leave, Momma Carrie yelled out the window, "Billy...go to your Uncle Buddy's and get your shit together." I was angry at my Mother for abandoning me and making me move. I felt like she had wronged me. My older self realizes that she did what she thought was right. I couldn't believe that she had kicked me out, but now, I understand why she did.

I was 19, sleeping on my Uncle's couch, helping my cousins take care of him. He was old and very sick, but well enough to frequent the racetrack. He loved horses and gambling. Even though I was underage, I would often accompany him to the track and place bets for him. On those trips to the track, Uncle Buddy told me a lot of stories about he and Momma's family. He talked about their upbringing in Oklahoma and North Carolina. The Watkins clan was a strong Black family that made it out of that terrible time in the South. He did his best to share the family stories and to help make me feel like it was a part of me. It just didn't work. I was a member of the family, but I knew that my DNA belonged in a pool of people that were unknown. I was a fish out of water. I started to resent him, and I had no further interest in learning about people that didn't share my blood. My innate response was to detach, and I became more and more lazy and despondent.

One day, in an effort to try to help me grow, my Uncle Buddy took me on a ride. I thought it would be to our usual racetrack, but this time, we made a B-line to Riverside Military Recruitment Center. I was sick to my stomach. My Uncle told me that this was the last stop to save me. He warned me that if I didn't enlist, my life would be marred, and I would likely end up in jail or dead.

The recruitment process was daunting. Since my past was such a secret, I didn't have any of my paperwork. I went to the office without a birth certificate, social security card, or any other identifying information. I couldn't answer any of the military questions related to my medical history. People like me struggle with simple tasks like filling out forms or answering basic biological questions. My Uncle Buddy couldn't answer the officer's questions either. The recruiting officer made a call to my Mother, and they talked for 5 minutes. Next thing I knew, I was taking a test, then told to choose Army, Navy, Air Force, or Marines. I chose the Army. I wasn't privy to the contents of the conversation, but whatever my Mother said was sufficient to get my recruitment approved almost immediately. I was sworn into the Army as recruit Billy Williams and was swiftly on my way to Fort Sill, Oklahoma.

I looked at this as an opportunity to change my life. Before this moment, I had a love for cocaine and its close cousin, acid. It served me for years and now, I had detoxed from both and surprisingly, passed the required urinalysis. I looked at passing the urine test as a sign to make a permanent change. I was 19 and had kicked a nasty cocaine and acid habit, cold turkey. It was overdue. I had made some terrible choices and hurt a few people. It was time to fix myself and my damaged relationships.

It wasn't easy, but I kept my body free from drugs and I felt like I had finally found a home. The Army made me feel like I had a reason to live. It gave me a purpose and I was committed to serve my country. I wanted to serve my friends back home in California, and to protect my family wherever they were in the United States. I learned early in this process that, even though I don't know who I am, the Army really doesn't care. The job isn't predicated on identity, because the military gives you a new identity and way of being in the world. The military only cares about what you're going to turn out to be, not what you were. Most recruits aren't soldiers when they get on base, but by the time basic training is over, they are transformed into true soldiers. My transformation was miraculous and exactly what I needed then.

Becoming a soldier was hard, but given the

events of my past and, most significantly, the sudden death of my Father, it wasn't the hardest thing that I had ever gone through. I hated the yelling and spitting that our drill sergeant spewed. I wasn't intimidated because I had taken orders from choir directors. There was nothing more intimidating and scarier than a church choir director like Don Lee White or Pastor Russell Thomas Hill. They had a look that would scare the devil and could launch a Daniel Green slipper or hymnal so far and hard that it could take out a misbehaving child's eye. A military drill sergeant would shutter with fear from the wrath of a church Mother.

Most recruits would complain about the mistreatment when we returned to the bunk. I would lay in bed and smile, thinking about those old church days. It was easy for me because I had experienced those church women, coaches, and the most fearful of them all, Momma Carrie.

I flunked the physical fitness test. There I was, a star athlete in football, I swam, rode horses, practiced martial arts for 13 years, and I couldn't pass the fitness test. I was so embarrassed. Everyone was moving on and I was still on the easiest part of basic training. I was crushed. My default response for failure would have been a line or two of cocaine. That was no longer an option. I had to manage failure in life like a man, not like a drug addict. My 6'3", 210 pound frame had gotten out of shape when I left college and all the drinking and smoking didn't help either. I didn't finish the running event at all, and I couldn't complete 13 military push ups. I was mentally defeated. I thought about going home, but that would mean doing drugs and collecting notches on my belt, all while sleeping on someone's couch. I was reminded that I had survived two-a-days in the blazing sun, running on the football field, with coaches pushing me to the brink of death. I didn't give up then, and I couldn't give up now.

The drill sergeant gave me 10 days to pass the fitness test. If I didn't pass, I would be sent home. I had already failed in college and now, I might fail the physical test to enter the Army. I would be devastated. There is no way I could face anyone if I failed this test. For the first time in a long time, I prayed. I had been trained to go to God in hard times, but I hadn't done so in a very long time. I asked Him to let me pass so that I could really see Him for myself. I thought He was real, but I had never experienced His power. I asked for strength to succeed in this test. Looking back, it seems so silly that I would pray to pass a fitness test, but passing would mean that God actually heard me. I didn't want to go home. I wanted something different. I wanted a life, and this test was going to be the catalyst to get one. Something inside of me told me that I would continue to battle the demons in my mind, until I totally surrendered to Him.

I didn't totally surrender right away, however, I started to realize that I had a Heavenly Father that was always with me. I didn't completely grasp the concept at first, but I started to see God in a way that I had never seen before. It was kind of weird. This invisible being, this Spiritual Father relationship, didn't feel like anything I had ever experienced. It was better than good.

After 9 days of good eating, great training, lots of prayer, and one day's rest, it was time to take the test again. I gave myself a pep talk and was reminded, in my spirit, there was nothing left but to do it. I started with the push up challenge. Taking powerful deep breaths, I completed those push ups with ease. Next was sit-ups, and then the 2-mile run. As I took off, I imagined myself running from my past and into my future. With every step, I released a bit of rage. With each breath, I breathed out drug and sex addiction. I was running for my life, and I wanted to be free. I passed the test with flying colors and was finally a soldier. The greater gift, however, was that I felt the power of God in real time, and He not only heard my prayers, He answered them.

Graduating basic training was one of the most satisfying feelings I've ever had. The joy, excitement, and satisfaction of completing the course gave me hope that I could accomplish anything that I set my mind to, and that God ordained for me. I was grateful I made it through the class. I was a soldier with a duty to serve my family, my friends, and my country. I took the job very seriously. I was no longer a person only concerned about me, rather, I was committed to represent the uniform that I donned. More than anything, I was proud that I had followed through with something. Up to that point, I was a rudderless ship, flailing about at sea with no destination. My past was no longer haunting me, but the desire to know who I was still lingered just below the surface of my newly constructed soul.

The day that I graduated, Momma Carrie, Aunt Gladys and my high school girlfriend all attended. I have always had support from Momma, as long as I was doing right. Six months before, she kicked me out of the house. Now, she stood proud of her son. All day she kissed and hugged me and told me how proud she was. I had done something that made her proud. I hadn't seen her glow since those old football days and marital arts competitions when I was a child. That day, as I stood in my dress uniform, posture straight as arrow, I was a man that finally made her proud. Looking up in the stands, seeing her beaming smile, I almost shed a tear. I gave her a thumbs up instead. I knew in my heart that this was the tip of the iceberg. I was determined to do something spectacular just like I had done while I was dominating on the football field.

In her own way, Momma taught me that good is rewarded, and bad will be punished, and my experience in the Army confirmed this. A lot of people may not agree, but the Bible is clear — righteousness will be blessed, and evil will be punished. I know the truth of this because I lived it. It was proved to me on a field at Fort Sill long after Momma Carrie and the church mothers taught me at Grant AME.

CHAPTER TEN

Man Up

When you don't have a Father, a man tends to overcompensate and indulge their children. I didn't know how to be a Father, but I knew I wanted children. In the end, I didn't marry my high school girlfriend, instead I married a woman who already had children. I was thrust headfirst into fatherhood. Not only where they my children, but during my military service, I decided to start coaching at the local recreation center on Fort Gordon Army Base, where I was stationed. I knew the impact that coaches made on me, and I wanted to give back.

One of my proudest moments was winning the 11-13 football championship sponsored by Omega Psi

Phi Fraternity, Incorporate. We won 3 years in a row. Every game, I wore a hat like Bear Bryant, the old Alabama coach. I wore a purple and gold long floor length coat that my wife made. I loved coaching those boys. Those kids trusted me, and we taught them strength and perseverance and to believe in each other. We were a well-oiled machine, working together. The team was made up of all races and colors. Coaching was my way of connecting as a Father figure to more kids than just my own. I wondered if my biological parents ever thought about me. I wondered if they longed to see me the way that I saw those children playing, carefree and happy. I wondered if they ever thought of me at all.

I had made up my mind that there was nothing I could do to discover the identity of my biological parents. It was time to grow up and let the dream of knowing them die. I had lived burdened by the secret of my roots for long enough. It was time to move on and resolve that I would never know who I came from. There was no need to harp on this anymore. I dove into doing my job as a soldier and through my efforts amassed a few medals for my service.

Army life is a very hard life to live. You are deployed a lot, unless you are one of the lucky ones who can stay back in a garrison unit that doesn't go anywhere. I had no such luck. I was gone all the time. I was part of a few rapid infantry deployment units, and then a combat stress medical unit. I always had to be ready to go within 45 minutes. I kept my deployment gear packed all the time. There were situations where I had to get home right away, kiss the wife and kids, and then leave to some exotic place without much forewarning. There is a certain mindset a military person and their family must have to be able to cope with the challenges military life brings. I love being a soldier. I say that in the present tense because we are taught that although you are not active in the Army, a soldier is a soldier for life.

While on deployment in Panama, I got injured. It was bad enough to require 4 surgeries, and it landed me in a wheelchair. The details of my injury are still difficult to discuss. The physical injury wasn't the hardest part to heal from. It was the mental anguish that sent me back into the darkness of drugs and homelessness. All of the spiritual and emotional progress that I had made vanished in the blink of an eye, and I was now a homeless, wheelchair-bound, drug addicted, Army Veteran. My shame had gotten the best of me, and I was reluctant to be around Momma Carrie. By now, she was in her 70s and I was of no use to her. I couldn't help myself and I certainly couldn't help her, plus, the son that caused her to beam with pride, was once again drug addicted, and now, stuck in a wheelchair. She had been working as a caterer all while I was squandering my life before the military, and she was now retired. I was able to push my shame to the side long enough to talk to her on occasions when she was in the hospital. It was easier to visit with her at the hospital because of the wheelchair. It was difficult, if not impossible to navigate her home in the chair, so even though I would have rather her not be in the hospital, I could at least navigate around her room to visit her. Those times that I could go to her house, we would talk in the driveway. We had a chance to heal from our past. She told me how sorry she was that she couldn't tell me more about my parents and she told me that she wished she knew more. I apologized for being an ass and she told me to watch my mouth. To this day, if a cuss word slips out of my mouth, I giggle and think of her. My Mother told me she understood why I acted out and she said that any normal person would do the same. In those moments, during those driveway conversations, I began seeing her for who she was, my Mother. She loved me and I knew it because she had always shown it. I was often just to blind to see.

It was awesome to have that relationship with Momma Carrie at that critical time in my life. I was very fragile. The wheelchair put a hurting on me, emotionally, mentally, and physically. Just as we were mending our collective broken hearts, my Momma went home to Glory. I was happy that we had the opportunity to talk and spend time together before she passed. Had we not, I'm not sure what I would have done. I had, in those dark days, contemplated suicide, but I never had the guts to carry it out. Truthfully, I was too afraid of where I would end up if I was successful. Not reconciling with Momma Carrie before she died might have taken me over the top. At her home going celebration I was able to read a poem I wrote for her:

** * **

Paradise

Looking forward to the cloud coming down from the sky, our souls rising, yes we can fly. On our way to paradise that's where the book lies. The Goal The Prize the Kingdom don't need no worldly freedom to free we are free in the holy trinity witnessing for the three for infinity headed for eternity, might be soon check a red moon like a rose in full bloom sudden boom upper room receive our robe our crown of life no more strife, envy, hate don't trip we hadn't ate. We're Full of His love, joy and His peace continuing to share in the everlasting feast. Walk the streets of gold, gaze at the jasper stone, singing in Hallelujah tone. This is our true paradise, our life, our vice, meeting face to face, Yeshua Jesus the Christ.

Momma dying was difficult but watching her suffer was harder. She died of Alzheimer's, and it took its toll. She lived a good life, and she gave her all to me and the church. She did her best to raise me right. She taught me love and lessons and tried her best to keep me on the straight and narrow. She ruled with an iron fist and loved me with her whole heart. Her death closed a chapter, but another one was beginning, and this one rocked my world in ways that I never thought possible. When my Mother died, I began to see the true colors of my family. I discovered that many people in my family didn't really love me, and several didn't even consider me Momma Carrie's son. When she died, I learned their obligation to accept me died too.

Soon after her funeral, I got a phone call. The person on the other end of the line was in a panic, "Billy you need to get over to your Mom's right now. People are taking all your stuff." I don't remember the whole conversation, but I do remember saying that they could take whatever they wanted. All I wanted was my adoption paperwork and any other paperwork that would help me discover who I am. My Mother had nice things. As a child, I would spend days cleaning the crystal glasses and trinkets that she had acquired. We had a beautiful piano and tons of furniture. There were sets of silver flatware and loads of china. I didn't care about any of it. All I cared about, all I wanted were the papers that would help me learn who I was. This was my one and only opportunity to learn and I wasn't going to miss it. The anticipation of knowing rose up in me and I was on a mission to discover my roots.

Momma never would have given me any of my paperwork. In fact, there were times that she would lie and say that she didn't have anything. I knew better. I had stopped asking her years before, but I knew that somewhere, in that house, the answers I sought were just waiting to be discovered. It sounds morbid, but I had to wait for my Mother to die before I could find myself. I prayed that I would finally get my birth certificate. I had so many questions that were about to be answered. I wondered if my birthdate was *really* my birthdate. Would this birth certificate show my biological mother's name? What about my biological father? Would it be there? What hospital was I born in? Where was I born? The questions that I had asked my whole life, that never got answered, were about to be.

As I arrive at the house, I took a deep breath as I worked my way in. I'd been in the wheelchair for a while and had learned how to get in and out of it, not with ease, but I did well enough. When I entered the house, a family member handed me a small brown briefcase. I was shaking as the cold leather rested in my hand. I breathed deeply, and opened the case. As the latched clicked free, I felt a rush of emotion. The pages shown bright white against the brown leather. So simple. Just a few pieces of paper could unlock a lifetime of mystery and wonder. I'm not sure if I, or someone else opened it, but the first thing I saw was a name, and it wasn't mine:

William Collins.

My name was William Collins. He was a stranger. I'd gone my whole life as Billy Williams. My military records said that I was Billy Williams. My social security card says Billy Williams. My driver's license says Billy Williams. Everything in the leather bag says my name is William Collins, and I began to wonder if the bag would cause more questions than answers. I thought that the adoption paperwork would help me. Rather, I was more confused than ever before. The brown leather briefcase revealed more. I located a baptism certificate that said that I was baptized Billy

Williams. I remembered this paper because I asked to be baptized when I was a child. I was later told that I was able to live as Billy Williams because of that baptism certificate. Back in the day, that's all you needed to provide a court or government agency to effectuate a name change. That wouldn't fly nowadays.

The briefcase held old football sports contracts that Momma signed giving permission for me to play because she was my parent, but nothing about my adoption. I found old report cards, and a letter to the school explaining why my name was Billy Williams and not William Collins, the person on the birth certificate. I guess with those papers, Momma Carrie was able to get me through the system.

I continued searching, but no adoption paperwork was found. The only thing other that my birth certificate that piqued my interest was a letter with Aunt Sayran's phone number listed.

William Collins

If that was my birth name, and that document was

real, I finally knew who I was at birth. I had been told that birth certificates could be falsified, though, so I didn't bank on the information. I couldn't imagine that anyone would falsify a birth certificate, especially in the 1960s. Thankfully, there was a letter confirming that I was the person on the birth certificate. I studied the document and discovered that I celebrated my birthday on my BIRTHDAY too! I was thrilled. I also learned from this birth certificate that my Dad was a Negro. I am Black! Thank God. I was just a little light-skinned, but I am still Black. For a split second, I wanted to find that kid from kindergarten and the announcer at the rodeo and show them that they were wrong! I am Black.

I also learned that my birthmother was white. A bi-racial baby, born in the 1960s at the height of the Civil Rights Movement, is what I am. I immediately thought about my birthparents and what it must have been like for them having a bi-racial baby during that tumultuous time of civil and racial discord. I imagined them as lovers with a forbidden relationship, and I instantly romanticized their union. The fantasy in my mind ran wild. It took me a while to embrace the fact that I was both White and Black, but that was the least shocking part of my story. Pandora's box had been opened and the secrets that would tumble out would be unbelievable and earth shattering.

CHAPTER ELEVEN

The truth, the whole truth, and nothing but the...

Now, finally, that story that I was the bishop's kid can be put to rest. I'm not the bishop's son. The people that grew up with me know which bishop it was too. I don't need to say anything, this rumor was legendary in the church, and now, it has been dispelled for good.

People didn't know how much this rumor bothered me. I didn't want to be a product of an affair, and certainly not one between my Mother and the bishop. Both would have been married at the time and I would have inherited the scarlet letter by default. It bothered me most, because if it was true, this man of

God rejected me as his son. The brown leather briefcase put all of that to rest and I didn't have to worry about that anymore.

Although this new information was good for me, I was still trying to recover from years of hurt and pain. I made it through many hard times already, and I was learning to deal with the wheelchair without having a steady residence. Sadly, I resorted back to what was familiar and began taking medication prescribed by my doctor. I was on a steady diet of Morphine, OxyContin, and Paxil, just to name a few. I was also smoking a pack or two of Newports everyday, and chasing it all down with a half a bottle of Crown Royal in the evening. People tried to make me feel bad because of what I was doing to myself. I was constantly reminded of the commitment that I had made in basic training when I decided to commit my life to Christ.

The guilt and shame had gotten the best of me, and I found myself buried in the Word, once again, looking for answers. I read where Jesus says in Matthew 15:11-20, *"Not that which goeth into the mouth defileth a man; but that which comes out of the mouth, this defiles a man. But those things which proceed out of the mouth come from the heart; and they defile a man."* People use what others eat, drink and smoke, even the consumption of drugs to condemn them, claiming they are sinning, and using God as back up for their condemnation. That's not God's character. He focuses on the heart of the man and wants to heal the source of sin. 1 Samuel 16:7 is clear, *"People look at the outward appearance, but the Lord looks at the heart."* We must know and understand what the Bible says, not what people tell you. This knowledge changed my life forever.

One day, I had a very eye-opening conversation with one of my nurses, Nurse Lee. She asked me if I wanted to die. I told her I wasn't sure, but that I was tired of the ongoing pain that I was in. Nurse Lee told me that it looked like I wanted to die. "You are gaining weight at an alarming rate and your lungs look and sound terrible." I suppose those cigarettes and ever-present drug use had taken their collective toll on my body. I had ballooned to 325 pounds, and I was hardly able to carry on a conversation without losing my breath. She said, "Billy, you are killing yourself. Is this what you want to do?" God reminded me of 1

Corinthians 10:23. It states that, that everything is permissible, but everything is not beneficial.

I didn't want to die, I just didn't know how to live. I had a choice to make, change my habits, or face the consequences. I chose to live and to stop doing the things that were killing me. That day, I quit smoking cigarettes. I started slowing down the drinking, and eventually stopped drinking all together. I was really trying to do better. I was still depressed because I couldn't walk and because of PTSD that I was suffering with because of my experiences in the Army, so my doctor kept me dependent on a cocktail of prescription drugs. I was also on the uptick financially. Momma Carrie had left me some money when she passed. My family challenged my entitlement to the inheritance because I wasn't biologically hers. Their threats and pronouncements hurt me deeply. The hope of being awarded tens of thousands of dollars would help me get a more stable living situation, pay for some much-needed school supplies, and allow me to start a savings account. I was hopeful and optimistic because things were beginning to look up. I was also keenly aware that another storm was raging and soon, it would make landfall in my life.

Reality set in when Momma Carrie's family took me to court to challenge my portion of the inheritance. I was devastated. They hired lawyers and everything. Well, they had a lawyer. I didn't have one because I couldn't afford one. Since there was no adoption paperwork, and the only evidence that I had that I was her son were football contracts where Momma signed her name as my parent, and my report card that said she was my Mother, were not enough to convince the judge that I was her son. None of those documents mattered. The judge said that there was no proof I was legally a member of Momma Carrie's family, and therefore, I wasn't entitled to anything from her estate. In my mind, this was crazy. My whole life this was my family. There were people in that courtroom that had whooped my butt, sewed clothes for me, and taught me how to cook. We played cards at family gatherings, and they watched me play sports. No one stood up for me. They all banded together and said that I wasn't Momma's son. Again, I was all alone in this world with no one to claim me.

As a result of their continued rejection of me, I

got angry at everyone in Momma Carrie's family, even the ones that say they had no idea I was going through this battle, or that they were shocked that the family was doing this to me. I was angry at the whole family. They knew I needed the help, but they still denied me what was rightfully mine. The blessing I thought I was going to get didn't happen. I could have resorted to the usual ebbs and flows of drug usage and depression, but this time, I channeled my anger, got in God's face in search of answers and guidance, and ultimately became an ordained minister. I didn't succumb to the pattern that I had set up decades earlier. I pivoted and stood faithful to the Word when the world (or at least my family) had left me. I landed a job at a high school coaching girls basketball and the varsity boys football team. I was committed to studying the Word and was doing my best to follow the teachings of Christ. I was enrolled in college and was doing well. I had no family, but I had God. I chose to stay strong. I chose to stay on course. I could have blamed God for the evil actions of others, but I didn't. They knew that I was entitled to my inheritance, and they knew I was Momma Carrie's son. They lied to the judge about who I was, and they have to live with the choices they made. I was free and my prayer was that they would find their own freedom too. I'm not sure they ever did. I've always been curious — how do they sleep at night? Always remember this: don't blame God for what other people do to you. People will answer to God for their terrible, dirty deeds. The Bible says so, and I know so.

As I continued my quest for happiness amidst the challenges, I got another letter. It was from my Daddy Bill's attorney. The letter stated that I was the sole heir of his estate. He left me, his son, an inheritance. To be an heir meant that I belonged to him. That realization, and the confirmation of that, changed my life. I wept with joy, partly because the money was needed, but more than anything, it meant that I was my Father's son. When one door closes another one opens, especially when you are doing right by God. What a trip? I had this money available to me years ago, but didn't know it. I guess it wasn't the time then. I probably would have smoked it up with rock cocaine anyway. But now, it was right on time. I didn't receive as much as I was going to receive from Momma Carrie's estate, but that didn't matter. I was my parent's son and the inheritance that I did receive was enough to continue my quest to live my better life.

CHAPTER TWELVE

Secrets and Lies

The brown leather briefcase held more than just my original birth certificate. It also held a letter that included the contact information for my Aunt Sayran. I decided that I would call her to see how she was doing. It had been decades since I last saw her, and I guess I wanted to connect with her as a by proxy way to connect with Momma Carrie.

When she answered my call, it was as if she was expecting to hear from me. She asked that I come visit with her because she wanted to share something with me, and she needed to do it person. I couldn't imagine what she would have to say, but I wasn't going to miss the opportunity to sit at her feet and listen, no matter the topic.

I hopped in my car and drove the 6 hours to get to her. During the trip, I fantasized about what she could possibly share with me. Maybe she had more pieces of information related to my adoption. Maybe she had paperwork for me. Maybe she just wanted to see her friend's son. Whatever the reason, I was determined to get to her, and a 6-hour drive wasn't going to stop me.

When I arrived, she met me with open arms. She told me that Momma Carrie made her promise to wait till she was dead to tell me how I came about. I asked her what the plan would have been had I died first, or worse, if she would have died before Momma Carrie. She said, "Baby, you would have been shit out of luck." I laughed so hard. She stood up, and stretched her back, then sat across from me on her sofa. "Billy," she said, "God wants you to know this, and God has something important he needs you to do." I got nervous. Aunt Sayran was serious, and her voice and countenance shifted. She looked deeply in my eyes, "God is going to use you and you must forgive your Mother for what she did. Do you understand?" I shook my head in agreement. My heart was racing. *What in the hell had Momma Carrie done? Who was I and how did she get me?* I broke out in a cold sweat and steadied myself to hear what Momma Carrie had sworn to keep secret until she died. Aunt Sayran began telling me the most fantastical story. I was left speechless.

According to her, one day my Mom called and told her that they had the opportunity to get a baby. She wanted to know if Aunt Sayran thought it was good idea. She said that Momma Carrie and Daddy Bill suffered with infertility. My Dad was on board with acquiring this baby, but Momma Carrie was nervous. Aunt Sayran told her that she thought it was a good idea. She told her, "Carrie, if you feel that this is the right thing to do it doesn't matter if he is White." A few days later, Momma Carrie and Aunt Sayran headed, by car, to Las Vegas to get me, the White baby. She said that they arrived at a seedy hotel and they were summoned to a room that had an adjoining door. When they walked in, a White man was standing off to the side. He approached Momma Carrie and handed her some papers. She looked over the papers and nodded her head. The White man went through the adjoining door and returned with a White child, me. Momma Carrie reached into her handbag and pulled out $10,000 cash and handed it to the White man. He then placed my hand in hers and vanished into the other room. Aunt Sayran sat in stunned disbelief. Momma Carrie stood up, grabbed me, and we all walked out as though the entire transaction was completely normal.

After she fell silent, my mouth was wide open. I tried to compose myself, "Wait. They bought me?" I couldn't believe it. "They bought me for $10,000?" She was tearing up, "Yes. Your parents paid $10,000 for you."

Everything, each word from that birth certificate came flooding back to me. It said that I was bi-racial. It said that I had 3 siblings. It said that my Mother was White and my Father was Black. And now, I discovered that I was bought for $10,000. That tripped me out. My birthmother sold me for $10,000 dollars. My White Mother sold her half Black child for $10,000. I was angry and confused. How could a Mother sell her son? And she had 3 other children.

That means that 3 other people knew about me. Were they sold too?

Aunt Sayran put her head down for a while. I think the gravity of what she said finally hit her. She eventually looked up. I looked into her eyes and asked, "Did she sell them too?" My Aunt assured me that she hadn't. "No baby, they went with your Mom back home to where she was from." I was even more confused and then an avalanche of emotions tumbled over me. "You weren't welcomed, and she sold you." Aunt Saryan was in a full cry at this point. I was dumbfounded. *What in the hell was happening in my life?* It was too much to process. I screamed, "Are you serious? I'm the only one that got sold?" I didn't wait for an answer. *Damn! Ain't this something. Why me? Why me?* "Why wasn't I welcomed?" I asked even though I knew the answer. She said, "She couldn't keep you because you are half Black." *What? She had slept with a Black man, but she sold her Black child? He was good enough to sleep with, but I wasn't good enough to keep.* I was enraged. Aunt Saryan kept apologizing. My whole life I wanted to know my story, but this was beyond my comprehension. I was SOLD.

I could feel her pain as she repeated the story. She said, again, that a tall White man came into the room and talked for a minute, asking if Momma Carrie wanted to do this. My Momma said yes, and then the man left and then he came back with me. They took me home, and everyone kept asking my Mom where I came from. She said people commented, "Carrie just pulled this White baby right out of thin air." She repeated the story 3 times. Each time I heard it, it was like I had never heard it before.

Aunt Sayran said that when they brought me home from Las Vegas, I cried a lot in the beginning, and it hurt their hearts to see me go through such a traumatic adjustment. I remember seeing pictures of myself in a crib and, in every picture, I was crying. I now understand why, I was with strangers. I wasn't with my Mom, I wasn't with my Dad, and I wasn't even with my 3 siblings. I was a baby who was ripped from everything I had ever known.

I asked how old I was when I was sold. Aunt Saryan put her head down again. "You were about a year and a half when your parents bought you." I was *over a year old.* Another body blow. I wasn't an infant when they bought me. I was a child, that was diapered, fed, and cared for by my birthmother for over a year. She bonded with me, and then sold me to the highest bidder. My siblings had to know about me. My birthfather had to know about me too. I wondered if they ever thought about me. I was the proverbial and literally Black sheep of my biological family.

I realized that the decision to sell me was one-sided. I asked Aunt Saryan, "What about my biological Father. Where was he and why didn't he take me?" She put her head down, brought it back up, looked at me and said, "He was gone baby. He was in jail." I was on the ropes and was sliding down to the mat, bloodied, bruised, and beaten. I was sold by a White Mother, and my Black Father was in jail. We chatted a bit longer, and then, I left. I knew the story, but I wasn't sure how to feel about it.

Learning my truth was a lot to deal with, but it explained so much. It made sense why Momma Carrie never answered my questions. I was a Black-market baby, the product of a street sale, sold under the table for ten grand. No paperwork exists related to the transaction. No one prepared a receipt and there was no return policy. I was a dark secret and now, I was on the hunt to identify the woman who sold me, and the man who fathered me.

Adoptees, or in my case, Black-market babies lack the simplest information. Most people can answer basic questions about themselves and their medical history, but we know nothing. In fact, until I was given my original birth certificate, I didn't even know my race. Now that I had my story, I was on a quest to find my biological family. I wanted to know my family history. I wanted to discover who William Collins really was.

CHAPTER THIRTEEN

Family Ties that Bind

During this time, I was just doing my best to live my life, focusing on getting closer to the only thing that has been constant in my life, my Father in heaven. My relationship with Him became my priority. I dove headfirst into studying God's Word on my own. I had pulled away from everybody, friends, family, and church members.

I had accepted the fact that I was in a wheelchair. I used the money that I inherited from Daddy Bill to buy a house. My fraternity brothers made it handicap accessible. I was living well, but I was lonely. I had no one to share my life with. I had a few failed marriages under my belt, one natural son, and I had 5 of my ex-wife's kids to care for, and provide emotional and social support.

With a history of failed relationships, I decided that I needed to begin praying to God and preparing myself for a wife. She had to be different, though. I had experienced so many bad relationships from my past, and I needed someone who could understand me and accept me and all of my baggage. She needed to be patient with me, and I wanted to be able to love again. I didn't think that anyone would want an emotionally damaged, former drug addict who was wheelchair bound. I had nothing to offer. God reminded me that I was His child and that He and He alone could help me find a wife. So, I began to pray.

Months later, just in the nick of time, my Father sent me my wife. She didn't care about my wheelchair or my past drug addiction. She was kind and gentle. She was focused on her own goals, and she inspired me to be my best self. I had never met anyone quite like her. She entered my life just when my doctors were going to readjust my pain medication. I was developing a dependence on them again, but my wife stepped in and warned me. She said that the pills were going to kill me, and I would lose her if I didn't stop. I argued and debated with her why I needed Oxy and Morphine in my life. I tried to make a case to justify my dependence to these drugs and she told me that the drugs were eating away at my body and they would eventually kill me. She had no intention of sitting around waiting for me to die. She gave me an ultimatum — drugs or her.

God reminded me that He had blessed me with who I asked for. She didn't care about my wheelchair, and she loved me and wanted to marry me. Just as clear as a bell, I heard the voice of God say, "She is your wife, and you are to heed her counsel. If you don't, you will die." I shudder, even now, when I think about those days. I got what I prayed for, and I was about to lose everything if I didn't surrender to God's Will.

With all the help my wife gave me and all the love she showed me, she still could not help me find my parents. She herself doesn't know the identity of her biological Dad. Honey understands the pain I was going through, and during the time that I was discovering my identity, Honey was grieving the loss of the only Dad she ever knew.

Instead of trying to figure out who I came from, I concentrated my efforts on the family I had in front of me. My wife and I didn't have any kids together, but she had three prior to me. This makes me a Father of 9. I did my best to teach them truth and honesty and to stand up to evil and to strive to live a righteous life. I think I did OK. One of my sons took my last name as his own because he says that I'm his Father. My son did the name change after I had to show him tough love like Momma Carrie had shown me. And like I did with Momma, he came back to me with Godly understanding and more love for me and himself than ever before.

My beautiful daughters, who love me as their Father, can't take my last name because they are already married. I instructed their husbands that my daughters are their wives, but they will ALWAYS be me daughters. Further discussion was unnecessary. My daughters are the joy of my life. After years of searching, I finally had a family, and I was content right there.

CHAPTER FOURTEEN
Chapter 11 Reorganization

Years past, and I was feeling wonderful. We had started a church, Unity Church, and we were a small, but thriving congregation. I had been in the wheelchair for 13 years, and with continuous rehabilitation and therapy, I had broken free from the ties that bound me to the chair. I was able to walk. It was a miracle! We, as a family, had gone through a great deal, but we were doing fine. I had long since kicked the drug addiction, once and for all, and Honey was excited about our future together, and so was I.

With the dust in my life finally settled, I began thinking about the missing pieces of my life puzzle. It started small, but the urge to know soon grew to an inferno that no water or prayer could quench. I wasn't actively looking for my biological family, but I knew that the time was coming to go from the comfort of one room, to enter the hallway where the mystery of my life resided.

On a whim, one of my cousins contacted me though FaceBook. We call ourselves cousins, even though we aren't related biologically or through Momma Carrie or Daddy Bill. We knew each other growing up in the church. She is the granddaughter of the Kidd family. I had worked with Paul Kidd in my teen years delivering BBQ sauce and our families were very close. I'm not sure how it happened, but we got on the topic of my family search. She told me she knew someone that could help me with completing my story. At first, I was skeptical. How in the world could a person find my biological family? I had searched for years, and was always left empty handed. There was no way anyone could find what I had been searching for my entire life.

My cousin gave me the phone number of a woman named, Shelbi Titus-Walker. Before calling her, I discovered that she was the founder of the

GRAITH Foundation, an organization dedicated to helping people connect with their family of origin. I called her. For the first 5 minutes, we made pleasantries. She was easy talk to and had a witty sense of humor. Her tone changed to a more serious one, and then she asked, "Now, Billy, what can I do to help you?" I was floored. No one had ever asked me if they could help me discover my story. I had been given breadcrumbs and scraps most of my life, so Shelbi's desire to actively help me, moved me to tears. I wept right then. I told her my story and at the end of my soliloquy, I breathed a sigh of relief. She breathed too. She asked that I provide her with everything that I found in the brown leather bag. "Now Billy, listen, I need to see everything. Don't sanitize the documents. The devil is the details. EVERYTHING is important." I honored her request and emailed her what I had. One day later, she went right to work.

I didn't make it easy on her at first. I think, to a certain extent, I was self-sabotaging the search. Something in my spirit knew that this encounter with Shelbi would be different. She couldn't make any guarantees, but I trusted her right-out the gate and I knew that she would find something. I wouldn't even do the DNA test. All she had was my birth certificate to go by. Her organization has been doing this work for over 20 years and she has solved over 1,000 cases. She is also a researcher for TLC Network's *Long Lost Family*, and she conducts workshops all over the country discussing topics related to adoption and unknown parentage. Unlike most researchers, she doesn't charge clients anything for her services. She is the real deal and is in high demand. I was grateful that she took my case.

I'm not sure how long it took, but within a few weeks of talking with Shelbi, she called me and told me that she had a significant update for me. I trembled when I heard her voice on my voicemail. As I dialed her number to call her back, I was shaking. I hoped that she had some answers for me. She answered the phone and said, "Billy? Are you sitting down?" I said that I was. "Well, I found your brothers. Not only that, I know where your birthmother is and, Billy, she's alive." I felt a cold rush through my body. I was glad that I was sitting down. I was trembling again and speechless.

I know some would be mad at her for selling me, but I wasn't. I just wanted to see her and know her. Her choice was already made, and it wasn't personal. I had to keep reminding myself of that fact. Shelbi told me something that stuck with me. "Billy, I believe that people are inherently good, they just make really bad decisions that impact the lives of others. Your Mother, I must believe, did the best she could with where she was. Approach this with the grace that God gives us every day." She was right. I had to deal with my birthmother with grace. I made the decision right then that I would be open to hear her story and not judge her for the decision that she made.

Late that day, Shelbi put me in contact with my brother. He was a decent guy. I told him that I was no Rockefeller but, I am rich in many ways. That first conversation was like gold to me. Through tears, he told me that he remembered me. I was nicknamed Junior. I was there with my brothers one day and gone the next. He always wondered what happened to his little brother. He told me he was in the military, just like me. Then, he said his daughter was also in the military. I was in awe of all of it. *I have a brother and a niece that were in the military.*

Sadly, he also verified everything Aunt Sayran said about the transaction. He also shared the reason that our Mother sold me. My Mother had been married and had my brothers. When she and their Father divorced, she was left to raise them by herself on a cocktail waitress's salary. She met my Father, and they had a love affair that produced me. When it became difficult for her to care for the four of us, she called her family in West Virginia. My Mother's White family didn't want anything Black in their family, and I was glaring reminder of my Mother's forbidden relationship. I was the family secret, and they wanted to bury the memory of me as far away as possible.

My brother told me that I had another brother on the West Coast, and that he had 3 children. Our other brother had died in a motorcycle accident years earlier. I cried for him. I had never met him, or even seen his picture, but I was sad that a part of me had died. It took me a minute to process that. Shelbi found the three siblings listed on my birth certificate. I had three brothers. When I asked about my Mother, he told me that my Mother was a minister. I screamed,

"I'm minister too!" I was so excited to talk to her. I couldn't believe that all of this happened so fast. I had waited my whole life for this moment, and now, it was here. My brother and I hung up after talking for over an hour, and I immediately called Shelbi. She was so excited for me, but she reminded me to take it slow. "Just because you have the same blood, doesn't mean you're the same. It takes more than DNA to make family." She was right.

At the end of our conversation, my brother agreed to contact our Mother, and then get back to me. I waited to hear back from my family. Shelbi and I stayed in touch as we waited. I was so excited. My wife and I were making plans to visit my new family as soon as possible. I wanted to meet them face-to-face. I would finally get to fill in another puzzle piece in my life. I wanted to meet her. I needed to meet her. Even though her decision was steeped in racism and bias, they were still a part of me, and I loved them.

About a week later, I got a call from my brother. His voice was soft and shaky. He told me that he had spoken to our Mother, and she said that she didn't want to speak to me. I was so confused. What was wrong? What happened? Are you kidding me? I couldn't believe it. She rejected me again. My biological Mother rejected me, again. What a gut punch. My own Mother had a chance to see the son that she cared for, the son that she diapered, the son she nursed, and the son she sold, and she denied me again. I was inconsolable. I didn't understand why nobody wanted me. I cried and cried for days. This was, by far, the worst part of my search. I had been rejected by friends, Momma Carrie's family, religious folk, but now, my own biological Mother has rejected me. Again.

My brother tried to console me and to soften the pain that I was experiencing, but it didn't work. I was crushed. Thank God my wife was there to hug me and tell me how much she loved me. Shelbi stayed in close contact too. She called me to reassure me that I was not responsible for my Mother's response. She reminded me that Jesus had been rejected too. That gave me a modicum of peace. Even though my Mother rejected me, my brothers and their families made me feel welcome. They stayed in contact with me through texts and phone calls, and they called me brother and Uncle. They always made me feel loved.

When the sadness of rejection subsided, I got angry. I'd waited over fifty years for this moment, for understanding, for completion, of meeting and knowing my people. I only wanted to get a hug from my biological Mother. Just a hug. Just a hug! I wanted to cry together and allow the tears to reconnect us as Mother and son. She was with me for over a year, and here I stood, 48 years later, waiting for her to love me again. I didn't care that she sold me. That was old news. I wanted to make the best of it, forget the past, and create a future. That is all I wanted. Just a hug. Just a conversation. Just a cry. I got nothing. The door to her heart was slammed closed and locked, and I was never going to get access to it. I wept again. Being rejected twice, in one lifetime, by my own Mother, what something I didn't think I would ever recover from.

My shock turned into anger. I wasn't expecting Christmas dinner, but a simple telephone conversation would have made all the difference in the world to me. She was a minister, but event the power of God couldn't even move her. She refused to meet with me.

Where was her faith and belief in God? I tried to justify her behavior. How would she explain me and her decision to sell me to her congregation? How do you tell people that you sold your Black son? Was I that disgusting to her? Was she that ashamed of me? Did I remind her of what she lived through? Was the sight of my face a reminder of a darker time in her life? Or was the shame so paralyzing that she couldn't bear to face it?

I tried to put myself in her shoes, but each time I thought about it, I got more and more angry. I'm sure she carried her decision with her every day. The burden of knowing what she did must have been suffocating, especially since she was a minister. Her shame had to have ground into her soul and her occupation may have been her attempt at redemption and seeking forgiveness. She knew me. I wasn't an infant who she had left at a hospital or fire station. I was her toddler son, who she brought to a Las Vegas hotel room to sell to strangers. This was her chance to heal and make amends. She didn't. Rather, because my Mother chose to protect her own feelings and totally disregard me and my feelings, for a second time, not giving a damn about me, the son she gave birth to, we never spoke to each other.

Two years later, I got a phone call from my brother. Our Mother had died unexpectedly. I never got to hear her voice, and she died with the veil of shame laying heavy on her soul. She never got the chance to meet me. I never got the chance to hug her. I never got a chance to say, "I love you." And she never got the chance to ask for forgiveness. The wound would have to remain open, unhealed, and raw. I had to learn to live with it as it was, and as it would be forever.

I will forever have that painful memory that my own Mother couldn't love me. She never defended me or stood up for me. Momma Carrie's family wouldn't stick up for me in court, now my own blood didn't and wouldn't stick up for me in this situation. Worst of all, I will always have the memory of being sold like a slave.

My biological Mother's family has been good to me. They invited me to her home going celebration in West Virginia. They included me in the obituary. I was listed as her son. They gifted me some of my Mother's belongings. My wife and I were also included in my niece's wedding. We had such a good time. We danced in a barn in Washington State, and I finally felt like I knew who I was. Honey and I truly enjoyed this beautiful family time.

Even though they tried to make me feel welcomed, it hurt so bad that my Mom didn't want to see me and that I would never be able to meet her on this side of Glory. It was the ultimate test of faith. I was putting into practice everything I had learned about the sovereignty of God. I don't blame her or my brothers. She, like Shelbi said, did the best she could with where she was. I had to believe that the shame that she carried prevented her from facing her truth. I understood that, even though I hated it.

Racism is shameful and I think that many members of my Mother's side of the family were racist. I love them despite their hatred of my DNA. They, with all their flaws and hate, are part of me. Their blood is my blood. It has been difficult to process this, and hard to embrace a people and a culture that purposely hurts, holds back, steals from, puts down, and allows unfair treatment of Black families all over this land. I'm at the stage in my life where, if you're not doing something productive to speak out against the treatment of Black people, then you must ratify the mistreatment of us.

It hurts me that the White blood that runs through my veins has a reputation of stealing from native people and killing Black people for no reason at all. They allow their own people to do terrible things against others with little to no consequences. It's also sad that even though I feel this way, no White person that matters cares enough to do anything about it. And yet, I am White. And I am Black. Reconciling the fact that I am both, and one rejected me because I was partially the other, baffles the mind. I didn't have a say or a dog in the fight. I am just the product of a sexual encounter between two people, yet I am the unfortunate beneficiary of their demons. Truth be told, only few people on my Mother's White side have ever reached out to me. I wonder if the others feel I'm not part of them because I am part Black. Or am I still a secret to them? It didn't matter. They were no longer a secret to me.

CHAPTER FIFTEEN

Him

I have had to continue this life living with rejection. I have a family that I must be there for and children that need a Father. I have a wife that needs her husband, and a grand baby that needs her Papa. I have brothers and sisters, nieces and a nephew, and a family that needs my prayers. I couldn't let the rejection by my birthmother stop me from doing what I was called to do. Her shame was not going to be my shame. I chose to live. The discovery of my Mother had taken such a toll on me, I decided that I should take a break from searching for my biological Father. For whatever reason, I was less concerned about him or his family rejecting me, but I wanted to take time to process all that had happened with my Mother before going down that road. Hindsight, they say, is 20/20 and looking back now, I wish I would have started the search for my Father sooner. Not taking that pause would have changed everything.

At the time, I really need the pause. I wasn't mentally or emotionally prepared to be rejected again. Shelbi was patient with me too. Every so often she would send me a text or an email letting me know that she was still available to help me find my birthfather. I appreciated her so much. I knew that when I was ready, she would be right there for me. But I wasn't ready to be rejected again. My Mother rejecting me was enough. I was tired of being hurt. Shelbi and my wife had been encouraging me for years to get a DNA test. It, according to Shelbi, could help us identify your race with a bit more specificity and other cousins that you may not know about. It could also be used to locate my Black family. I refused to do the test, much to their disappointment.

In and effort to help me get my feelings out, I started to write down my life story. I needed to pen words so that I could get ready for the next chapter of my life and to release the pain that I had experienced. Writing was cathartic and it allowed me to talk about things that I needed to get out. I knew that I didn't have all the information to complete a book, but I just started writing.

I started accepting God as my Father and my Mother. Over the years, I have seen God work. I've seen Him heal and deliver. He has answered so many of my prayers. He told me in His Word, in Matthew 12:46-50. "Who is my Mother? And who are my brothers?" Verse 50 says, "For whoever does the will of my Father in heaven is my brother and sister and Mother." This is the model I have taken on. If you are of God, and you are doing His Will, then we are family. I had no one to listen to except the Bible, so I started believing it, really believing it. Every time a person tells me something and they claim it's what the Bible says, I must go behind them and look it up for myself to make sure what they said coincides with what God said.

What I found out is that most people are only reciting statements or sayings that they have heard from others. Perhaps it is a catchphrase from a minister, a parent, a bishop, a pope, a priest, but it's not what God says. I know the Word because I read it for myself. With all the Bible apps that are available, there is no longer an excuse for you not to study on your own. You can query any subject or word, and the app will bring up the scriptures you need. All you must do is read them and then apply them to your life. Doing this will keep you from being deceived, like many who are traveling on that wide road getting ready to go through that wide gate that leads to destruction. I encourage you to use your Bible so that you can experience the joy and peace that I now have. You must experience Him for yourself, or your mind will revert back to the false teachings you have heard over the years. We are responsible for our own salvation, don't put it anyone else's hands.

CHAPTER SIXTEEN

Running a Race

A few years went by, and I was about halfway done with the book. I tried to tell myself that I was done with my journey for my identity. I felt like my story was over and I was ready to share it with the world. I convinced myself that I didn't need to dig deeper into my roots and discover my birthfather. I figured I would use the name that was on the birth certificate and then end my story there. It was already a pretty good read, I didn't needed any more drama or rejection. As with most things in life, man plans, and God laughs. As much as I didn't want to do the DNA test, the Lord kept telling me to do it.

A DNA test was the final step to me finding my

biological Father. With this information, I would be complete, and, in turn, the book would be complete too. It was the last step in a very long journey. Shelbi was always there for me and Honey through this process. When I made the decision to take the DNA test, she was willing and able to help me find my birthfather. She would use the results from test and the data that we had from the contents of the brown leather bag to identify him. I couldn't help but worry about what I would find on the other side of the test. Would he reject me too? Did he even know I existed? My mind was swirling, then, the results came through.

Fifty-nine percent European and 41% Sub-Saharan African. I also had a sprinkle of Jewish blood in there too. I'm an African Jew! It was incredible. I finally knew who I was and what I was. I was beyond excited, and I called Shelbi. We talked for a while and discussed my racial makeup. Most of my DNA was European. I had been told my whole life that I was too Black to be White and too White to be Black. I discovered that I was both, and that my racial identity was determined by my DNA, but my personal identity was mine to determine. I was, and still am, a Black man who just so happens to have European blood running through his veins. The more pressing issue that I was faced with was whether my Black Father would reject me like my White Mother. I couldn't endure anymore of that, but I knew that I had to finish this race. The Bible reminds us that, "The race is not given to the swift or the strong, but to the one who endures to the end." I had to finish, even if I didn't want to, I had to. It was time for me to find the source of my 41 percent.

Since I'm a follower of Christ, I love the fact that I'm part Jewish. It blows my mind, however, that Momma Carrie knew somehow to keep me involved with Jewish people throughout my whole childhood. We would often the visit The Temple on Olympic Blvd. in Los Angeles. She would just drop me off and the Rabbi would take me to services. She must have trusted them because she took me there all the time. Little did she know, she was cultivating my Jewish roots. I loved going there and now, having learned that I'm part Jewish, was awesome.

CHAPTER SEVENTEEN

The Point

So what is the point of this book? What is the moral of this story? What are the lessons we need to take from these experiences? To start off, you must learn early you are responsible for you. At the earliest point, you can start loving yourself. Get to know who you are and what you want. Get a purpose right away and listen to the voice of God.

As soon as you can, be protective of yourself, because you are important. You matter. You are needed. I don't care what the enemy says, you are a tool that God can use to bless others. Protect yourself until the people around you show you how they are and show you how they are going to treat you. After they show you who they are the first time, believe them, as Maya Angelou says.

Read! If you read, you can learn to do anything. You can learn to fix anything. Once you learn to read, read things that will build you up, teach you, and help you with living life. Read things that will bring you to the truth. You must learn to read so you can read God's Word for yourself. It's not hard, it's not confusing, you must believe what it says. This will be the most important read of your life. Just as my Aunt Clara stressed to me all those years ago.

Listen to God and ignore the enemy. How do you know the difference in the voices? The enemy's voice is meant to harm you. It will use your past against you. It is always putting you down, and will focus on the negative of the situation to convince you to quit. It is always telling you to go against God and go against righteousness.

God's voice is encouraging and positive, and tells you to continue striving. It will tell why you must continue. It will motivate you, and give you strength. Truth be told, that voice is God, our Father in heaven.

This isn't in any particular order, because you

need to learn to do all of this as soon as you can. Once you get this, don't let one person change your mind. Keep your mind focused on Jesus. Keep your mind and thoughts on God the more we do this, the easier life will be.

Be honest, first with yourself and second with the world. Have the courage to be truthful even if it hurts. God requires us to be honest. Every time we are dishonest, it adds consequences to our lives. As the consequences add up, life becomes more difficult.

Have your own life experiences. Live for yourself. Will you make mistakes? Yes. So what? They will be your mistakes to learn from and grow from. Yours. Soon you will see yourself making fewer and fewer mistakes.

Don't hurt the ones you love. When you hurt the ones you love, you create guilt within yourself. All forms of guilt turn into depression. And depression leads to death.

If you really love someone, show them. I Corinthians chapter 13:4-8 is clear. "Love is kind and does not delight in evil but rejoices in truth." Know that love is an action word. We, in every family, all over this world, need to implement this concept of love as a universal guideline, by which to live.

One of the most important things to understand is that you are responsible for your own salvation. As soon as you learn right from wrong, you are responsible. Don't allow your spiritual life or death to be controlled by someone else. Establish a personal relationship with our Father in heaven as soon as you can. Learn to depend on Him, and learn to stay connected to God.

Stay the course. Once you get on the narrow path, stay on it. Don't veer, don't waver, don't turn off at the fork where the wide gate is. Yes, there will be hills and valleys, some not self-created, sometimes the evil one will test us, but we must stand up to those tests. Study the temptations of Christ when Satan tempted Him. We are to handle Satan as Jesus did. Yes, you can stand up to evil. Yes, you can stand up to the devil. Stay the course.

These are just a few things God has taught me as a result of the life I've lived. In the Bible there are over 1,000 commands in the New Testament that will help you live the life God has for you. You can get a copy of them from the Christian Assemblies International web page. They have all 1,050 New Testament commands. In the introduction to the website it reads:

These commands cover every phase of man's life in his relationship to God and his fellowmen, now and hereafter. If obeyed, they will bring rich rewards here and forevermore. If disobeyed, they will bring condemnation and eternal punishment.

One last thought that came to me as I was finishing my writing. I, by no means, think of myself as equal to Christ. He was and is the Son of God and is perfect in every way. What I do know, however, is that when I find myself feeling down about how I came into the world and the circumstances in my life, I am reminded that me and Jesus have one more thing in common. We were both sold. The great news is that the cost that He paid for me was more than $10,000. He paid for my salvation with His blood and because of that, I was never lost.

CHAPTER EIGHTEEN

DNA

Once the DNA results were in, I knew that things were going to move fast. Shelbi has been involved with thousands of cases and her process is very methodical. She always says that, "In this business, you can't be wrong." She takes her time and crosses every T and dots every I. I, on the other hand, was pumped and I rushed into communicating with my DNA matches. She told me to slow down and consider the consequences before diving in. I didn't listen. I began contacting all of the Black matches on my DNA list. I don't remember how many emails I sent, but I was reaching out to everyone that looked Black or who shared DNA with someone on my list that was Black.

Not many returned my emails, but one did. It was a 4th cousin match, and because our relationship was so remote, they couldn't provide me with any information about my Father. I was discouraged, but not deterred. We waited for Shelbi to analyze the DNA and help me find my Father.

It didn't take long. Right away I noticed a 1st cousin had responded back to me. Shelbi had told me that DNA relationships on Ancestry are general and that sometimes a 1st cousin isn't a 1st cousin at all. It didn't matter to me. The DNA was a match and the person responded to me. I told Honey that the person had to be a pretty close relative to me. I knew the complexity of this information from Momma Carrie's family and from the last research Shelbi did on my Mom's people. I quickly told Shelbi, and she was so happy for me. But again, she told me to slow down to make sure that we are on the right page. She has experienced horror stories when it comes to DNA matches and making these discoveries. She is a stickler for protecting her clients and ensuring the accuracy of the information. I understood, but I was losing patience.

I was ecstatic that I had found a family member on my Dad's side after 53 years. 53 long years. I couldn't wait to talk to them and see what they knew about my birthfather. I finally connected with the Black side of my people.

I contacted the person that was listed as my 1st cousin. Turns out he's not my first cousin, but rather, my nephew. I discovered that I had a nephew on my Dad's side. This meant that I have a brother or a sister. After a brief conversation, I discovered that he is my brother's son. I have another brother. My nephew told me that my brother passed away 2 years ago. I was crushed because I knew when he said it, that if I would have done the DNA test when Shelbi and Honey were encouraging me to, I would have found my brother before he passed. I was heartbroken. My nephew tried to make me feel better by telling me that there was no guarantee I would have connected because he didn't submit his DNA until his Father died. I knew better. Shelbi would have found him, and I would have met him. She is an expert researcher and I have no doubt that she would have been able to find my brother, even if the matches were remote. She works wonders.

She has a gift and a calling to connect people to their family.

After a hearty cry, I accepted the fact that my brother is gone, and I could have seen him before he died. My nephew told me all about his Dad, my brother. He also told me about his grandfather, my Father. Was he really in jail? If so, why? Why didn't he take me? Did he know about the $10,000? Was he ashamed of me too? I was finally going to get the answers that I desperately needed. Answers that I sought my entire life. I was going to finally find out about my Dad, at least I hoped I would.

Unfortunately, my Dad died in 1981. I was 14 years old. Daddy Bill died in 1977. Both of my Dad's died within 4 years of each other. I had to come to terms with the fact that I was never going to meet my biological Father, and that hurt me to my core. It's a shame that after this long journey, I still didn't get a chance to meet my Mother or my Father. You would think that I would be angry about it, but I'm not. I completed my search and I felt like the race was over. I had accomplished what I set out to do, and now, I needed to live.

My nephew told me that I needed to talk to his Mom about my brother and my Dad. He told me that my brother was in the military. I learned that I have a niece and a sister-in-law. We immediately decided to have a Zoom call so that we could see each other. Days before our meeting, I felt like a child waiting for Christmas. I could hardly sleep. I was going to finally meet my Father's side of the family and they wanted me in their lives. I was wanted.

I had to wait 4 days for this meeting to occur. The suspense and my nerves were crazy. My wife and I took a drive to waste time as I waited for the meeting to start. I always found peace when I drive, and it was exactly what I needed to calm my nerves. It calmed me down and focused my spirit on the lovely scenery that God placed on the earth. We ended up on the Air Force base and stopped at the park. It was an awesome feeling to get to the place where a prayer I prayed as a kid was now being answered by my Father in heaven.

This is why you have to stay the course. God will answer your prayers, but sometimes it may take a little time. On many occasions over my lifetime, my prayers took a little extra time to be answered, but when God was ready, He answered each and every one in His own way. Are there prayers that haven't been answered? Yes of course, and some prayers are never going to be answered. I prayed to be able to hug my biological Mother. She refused, and I never got that hug. Some prayers don't get answered, but it's OK, you have to move on. You must find a way to continue to move forward, trusting that God's Will is greater than your own.

Shelbi had set up the Zoom. I invited her to participate because, without her, I wouldn't know where I would be. My brother's wife, my niece, and my nephew were on the call. It was an awesome moment. They told me how great of a person my brother was and how he would have loved to meet me. They teased about not knowing if he had any other siblings, but if he would have found out about me, he would have been elated.

I mustered up the courage and asked that dreaded question about my Dad being in jail. To this day, I don't really know why that was so important. I think it's to vindicate Momma Carrie. She finally told me, after 17 years, that he was in jail, but I didn't believe her. Honestly, I didn't care about the jail thing. I would have gone and visited him if I knew where he was. He was still my Dad.

My sister-in-law told me that my Dad was involved with some illicit conduct that landed him in jail for a short time. He wasn't in for long, but he was incarcerated when I was with my birthmother in Las Vegas. Momma Carrie was wrong. She was under the impression that my Father was in jail a long time, but he wasn't. By the time Momma Carrie told me he was in jail he had already been released and had been dead for three years.

I still don't understand what the big deal was. My birthfather wasn't the terrible criminal everyone made him out to be. I'm not sure about his morals or his values or how he was living, but that didn't matter either. He was a Black, male nurse in the 1960s. Knowing that I came from a man that had chosen a field that helped people, helped me to understand my own mission to help others. He accomplished a goal, and I must have inherited that gene from him. I must accomplish every goal I set for myself. I did it when I was in kindergarten, I did it during the fitness test at

Fort Sill, and I did it again. I found my family and myself. I didn't give up. I found the truth about God, the truth about me, the truth about the church, the truth about religion, the truth about my ancestors, and the truth about life.

Momma Carrie could have told me the truth when Daddy Bill died when I was 10. I asked her to find my birthfather. I begged. I cried. I pleaded and she didn't. I think that it was all too much for her to take. She couldn't understand why I needed to know so badly, but I did. I often wonder how different my life would have been if I knew then about my roots. Perhaps the bumps and bruises would not have been as severe. Perhaps I would have been happier. It doesn't matter now. The life I had was the one that I was supposed to live.

No one knows if my birthfather got any of the $10,000. We don't know if he was in cahoots with my birthmother, or if he even knew I existed. We don't have a clue what his mindset was. He was sick towards the end of his life, and he took his thoughts to his grave. No one on my birthfather's family knew about me. I was a secret of the family, one that was supposed to never be found.

When I think about it more, both families, Black and White, agreed to keep me a hidden. I can't be mad about one over the other, but it's a trip how it took me, a half-breed mixture of European and African descent, to bring two families one White and one Black, together, even if it was just for one night to conceive me. My Mom's side of the family kept me a secret because I was Black. I'm curious as to why I was such a secret on my Dad's side. Why didn't he tell somebody about me? Again, I will never know.

Although this experience didn't pan out like I wanted it to, it has given me a great deal of closure. This quest to find my parents started on that playground at 5 years-old, and ended in the desert when I was 53. That's a lot of years to look for something. A lot of years to have to deal with roadblocks and rejection. The ups, the downs, the valleys that seem to always show up. A lot of years to deal with teasing, from every direction, about who I was as a person. I was put down, and talked about behind my back, just for being who I am. I've been cussed out, yelled at, lied to, lied on, misunderstood, mis-quoted, ignored, stolen from, rejected, cheated, and violated. All of this, then God reminds me what Momma told me at 5 years-old when she was whooping my butt all the way home from that fight — "they talked about Jesus and they are going to talk about you." They did bad things to Him, they will do bad things to you. She was right. The more I choose to follow God and Jesus's teachings, the more people try to hurt me. I have my own secret though. God loves me and He has never left me, so I get the victory no matter what.

My prayer is that through my experiences you will achieve your goals and that my life will help you to dodge as many pitfalls as possible. Learn from my mistakes, and don't wait. The longer you wait to change your situation, the longer it will take to get through all of the consequences.

CHAPTER NINETEEN

My Petition

This is My Petition to all of my families, and to all families over the world.

To my White family, I love you! The point of this book is to let you all know this. I don't care about you being White. I love all of you, the ones I have met and the ones that still don't know anything about me. I pray this book can unite our families by correcting the painful past it began with. Join with me to forgive our family for their past and let's move on together, let's move on in God's love.

I promise not to hold you accountable for past

family actions, and to not blame you for the actions of White people all over the world. I will only treat you as I want you to treat me — with love.

To my new Black family, I love you. The reason for this book was to let you know this. I will not hold you accountable for what my Dad did. It's not your fault. I love you all, the ones I've met and the ones that I have not yet had the opportunity to meet. I pray this book can unite our families by correcting our painful past it began with. Join with me to forgive our families actions and let's move on together in God's love.

I promise not to hold you accountable for past family actions and to not blame you for the actions of Black people all over the world. I will only treat you as I want you to treat me — with love.

To Momma Carrie's family, I love you all. It's not your fault what I went through. I was sold into your family, but Momma Carrie and Daddy Bill paid for me to be in your family so I deserve to be in our family. I'm sorry if I blamed you at first for the evil your elders did to me. Please forgive me and receive me as your own.

Join with me to forgive our families for the

ongoing lies that have been told, and let's move on together in God's love. I promise not to hold you accountable for past family actions and to not blame you for the actions of Black people all over the world. I will only treat you as I want you to treat me — with love.

I also believe I have a mission to unite the human race. I think this is what my Aunt Sayran was talking about. I know it sounds crazy, but I do. I feel my life has a purpose and it wasn't just to go on a quest to find my birthparents, it was much more than that. My life and the life you are living is meant to accomplish one goal — God's Will. To start, I want to unite all three of my families. Wouldn't it be awesome to erase all the secrets, all the hate, with a family united in love? I want to have, Lord willing, a big family reunion, with all my families, all three. Including Iris and Uncle Martin's family. We are all connected through me. We could do this, and we should document it as a start to the healing of the world. Starting with our families first.

And think about this, we all are already connected with our military service. My brother, his wife and my nephews served in the military covering my Dad's side, my brother and niece served in the military on my Mother's side, and I served in the military covering Momma Carrie's side. So, we are already family due to our military service. Our military brothers and sisters are united worldwide. We are connected through our service. We can make a change for the better, we can eliminate the evil past and replace it with new family love. Who's with me? It won't be easy. Evil is strong, but not stronger than our Heavenly Father. Again, who's up for the task?

I know some of you are wondering how we can do this. I've thought of that too. One, we must find common ground in two things. One is in love. We have to find a way to love one another. Most religions require love so let's start there let's enforce love. Let's start by allowing people to be people as long as they are not committing crimes, let them be. We may not agree on each one's lifestyle, but, that doesn't give us a right to be evil to that person or evil to people that don't live like we do or understand like we do. God requires us to love them.

Righteousness can be our other common

ground. All we must do is agree that doing what is right and standing up to evil will be our new gold standard. Our fight, in this world, is against evil, not each other. It's not about White it's not about Black it's not about any race at all. It's about unity in righteousness.

How do I know? I don't hate the White in me and I don't hate the Black in me. I love all of me. The White in me is a Godly man and the Black in me is a Godly man. I love all of me because of the righteousness of God in me. If every person did their absolute best to live in righteousness and Holiness like God asked us to, and if each race, color and creed, stood up to the evil in their cities and corrected the evil in their paths, our world would be in a place of healing. This is my goal to start the healing process. This healing, beginning with righteousness and Godly love, is the key to a better world.

Who am I? A child sold in a hotel room. Who am I? I'm Billy Williams. Who am I? I am William Collins. Who am I? The son of a White woman. Who am I? The son of a Black man. Who am I? I'm European. Who am I? I am an African. Who am I? A husband, father, brother, uncle, cousin, and son. Who am I? A Pastor. Who am I? I am a Child of God conquering lies with His Word of truth, and it's been a pleasure to introduce myself to you.

9 780578 373751